DEEP SCIENCE IN ANCIENT INDIAN PHILOSOPHICAL THOUGHT

Deep Science in Ancient Indian Philosophical Thought

Anil K Rajvanshi

MOTILAL BANARSIDASS
INTERNATIONAL
DELHI

First Edition : Delhi, 2026

ISBN : 978-93-47683-88-6

Also available at
MOTILAL BANARSIDASS INTERNATIONAL
H.O. : 41 U.A. Bungalow Road, (Back Lane) Jawahar Nagar, Delhi - 110 007
4261 (Basement) Lane #3, Ansari Road, Darya Ganj, New Delhi - 110 002
203 Royapettah High Road, Mylapore, Chennai - 600 004
12/1A, 2nd Floor, Bankim Chatterjee Street, Kolkata - 700 073
Stockist : Motilal Books, Ashok Rajpath, Near Kali Mandir, Patna - 800 004

Printed in India
MOTILAL BANARSIDASS INTERNATIONAL

Preface

Ihave always been intrigued by the deep science embedded in ancient Indian philosophical thought. Whether it is Patanjali Yoga Sutras [1]; Gita; Sankhya Philosophy [2]; Upanishads; etc. - all of them contain some gems of fundamental science if we study them deeply and read between the lines.

Too often the ancient Indian scriptures were interpreted as simply a treatise on how to live properly but I feel the authors of these documents were great scientists or could have even come from other planets [3]! And with time the deep science was lost or misinterpreted, and lot of sutras or shlokas were omitted since the subsequent commentators did not understand the science. This book is my small attempt to address this issue.

The starting point has been Patanjali Yoga Sutras (PYS) [4]. I believe it is one of the most scientific ancient texts and probably the distillation of all the knowledge about mind, space and time that existed at that time. The science embedded in PYS is remarkable and most of the material described in this book constantly alludes to it.

One can ask a question; why are we interested in finding science in ancient scriptures? Some even can say that we are unnecessarily interpreting the sutras or shlokas and trying to embed science in them when it did not exist. Or we are just doing it to glorify the ancient Indian thought.

I feel that the natural course of evolution of human-like forms and beings is galactic travel since this is a part of experience gain and enlightenment. We are following this route. As we advance technologically, galactic travel is the next frontier, and we are following that goal.

It is my belief that this planet was seeded periodically by evolved humans who came from a technologically advanced civilization and another planet. That might partly explain the cause and reason of such a huge human brain.

Evolutionary forces could not have produced such a brain size on this planet. Subsequently these extraterrestrial beings may have mated with humanoids who evolved on this planet earth.

If this thesis is correct, then the ancients wrote about the accounts of science and space travel. And those are found in the scriptures. With time, this knowledge got reduced, diluted and corrupted. But what we see today are the glimpses of those great ideas of science regarding time and space.

Hence, by reading between the lines, we may be able to gather some hidden gems from these ancient scriptures which might help us to find new scientific laws, inventions and discoveries. That is the reason why we are interested in reading these scriptures and interpreting them in the light of modern science and technology knowledge.

The comparison of information in scriptures with modern science is neither to glorify our ancient tradition nor to belittle the latter – both are important in their own way; but to show that all great knowledge originates from the same knowledge space [5] irrespective of the person and the time of its discovery.

However, there are strange descriptions of weapons with extraordinary powers in Mahabharat [6] and flying machines in Ramayana [7] and other scriptures but there is no clue about the design of these technologies – just descriptions. Though they are fascinating things but is not the subject of this book. I have therefore focused on the ancient knowledge which we can evaluate in the light of present science and technology and use them in the present context.

My desire to present this line of thinking evolved slowly over time. As I read more deeply into these ancient books, I realised that there are some great scientific truths and knowledge which have remained hidden. The desire to unearth them is the subject of this book.

I have been writing on these issues since early 2000 [8] and hence thought of putting most of them in one place. I have selected a few of my articles which give the essence of the thesis. What I have written is the tip of iceberg. The ancient Indian philosophical literature is vast and to delve deeply and read between the lines in all of them is beyond the scope of one's lifetime.

Very often one has a desire to look at the ancient texts and subjects from the modern perspective. Newton spent half his life trying to decipher Bible from the perspective of his knowledge at that time. Similarly, we are fascinated by great works of Panchatantra[9]; Chanakya[10]; Kalidas[11]; Shakespeare, among others and try to see how they fit in our present scheme of things.

The value of ancient books becomes manifold when they can explain the situation in modern world. This is the motive of writing this book. As an engineer I have always tried to interpret ancient texts with the knowledge of existing science and technology.

All books have an element of biographical material in them. This is no different. This is my eighth book. I have written about the issues of spirituality and technology in many articles and books and writing this book has made me reflect on my life [12] and the forces which made me write such books on spirituality [13]. Most of the material for my books on this theme have come from the diary of ideas that I have regularly written since 1977 [14].

All the articles presented in this book have also helped me develop a new line of thinking and a mantra: Spirituality + Technology = Sustainability and Happiness [15]. I feel this provides a new paradigm of development not only for India but for the whole world.

Structure of the Book

The book is divided into two sections. *The first is the theme section* where topics like deep science in Patanjali yoga sutras (PYS) are analysed (part I). Patanjali always talked about mind and thoughts but did not talk about the origin of thought. So, part II deals with the nature of thought, its production, transmission and interaction with matter. We also get the glimpses of these ideas in PYS, and they are alluded in appropriate places.

The whole basis of Indian philosophy is to remove pain which is achieved by *moksha* or liberation from the cycle of birth and death. Part III discusses the issue of death from a scientific point of view based on the removal of neural and cellular memories from the body so that the fear and pain of death is reduced. This section also relates to death theme in some scriptures.

In all Indian philosophical books, there are always detailed descriptions of how to live a good life for ultimate liberation. Section IV describes one such paradigm of living and development based on modern science and technology and how it relates to the ideas found in scriptures.

There are overlaps in the subject matter of theme articles since they were written as standalone and in-depth articles. I have left them as they are since each theme is self-contained.

The second - general section contains essays which are also standalone and complement the articles in the theme section. These essays point out certain aspects not covered in the theme articles. And they are arranged in chronological order of theme articles.

All the references are given in the QR code which can be found at the end of each chapter. By clicking on the links readers can access them.

And it is my fond hope that interested readers may be inspired to undertake their own study of ancient texts in the light of framework outlined in this book.

Happy reading.

Anil K Rajvanshi
February 2026

Contents

Themes

  I. Understanding Deep Science
     in Patanjali Yoga Sutras 3

 II. What is Thought? Physical and
     Neurobiological Basis of its Production,
     Transmission and Interaction
     with Matter 21

III. What is Death and Can We Reduce
     its Fear? 60

IV. How Technology Guided by Spirituality
     Can Lead to Sustainability and
     Happiness — A New Paradigm
     of Development 77

General Section

  1. Ancient Indian Philosophers
     Understood Time Just Like
     Modern Physicists Do 95

  2. How All Great Discoveries are
     Spiritual in Nature 99

  3. What is Consciousness? 105

  4. Genesis of Fear and How to Reduce It 109

5. Nature of Form – Why Life is Attached
    to It? 114

6. Why Life? – And its Purpose 119

7. Science of Pranayama 125

8. How Sinuses May Help in Humming 132

9. Lessons from India's Spiritual Tradition 135

Epilogue 140

Acknowledgements 143

About the Author 144

Themes

The Deep Science in
PATANJALI
yoga sutra

Understanding Deep Science in Patanjali Yoga Sutras

Sage Patanjali has been my teacher. Whatever little I have written in the last 20 years on spirituality [1] or thought about the interaction of mind-matter [2] and higher things have been inspired by Patanjali's Yoga Sutras and I have always felt that his spirit has guided me in this journey.

Yoga sutras is basically a book of life or how to maximize your living potential. It also teaches little bit of Hatha Yoga but the most important lesson it teaches is how to make the mind (the instrument of comprehension) very powerful so that it can comprehend any secret of the Universe.

According to me Patanjali was a true scientist who gave the first knowledge about the control of thought and mind and about universal laws governing time and space. Unfortunately, till now none of the commentaries on Yoga Sutras have explored them through the lens of science. I feel this essay will help overcome that lacuna.

His writings are like an infinite ocean. The more you read them the deeper is the knowledge. Consequently I have made a small attempt in trying to understand their science through the publications of my two books; Nature of Human Thought [3] and Exploring the Mind of God [4] and this article is an attempt to explore it further and in depth.

Who was Sage Patanjali?

We do not know who Patanjali was [5] or when he wrote the Sutras or *even what we have today are really his Sutras;* but reading between the lines or extracting knowledge from them shows the great understanding and sparkling wisdom of his science.

Though we will never know the truth of his existence but his science-based teachings (Sutras) which were written *more than 2000-3000 years ago meant it must have come from a person not of this world!* I therefore feel that he may have been an astronaut from an advanced civilization [6] who came to this world to impart great scientific knowledge. This speculation is explored in a later section.

Thus, whether it is the definition of time, or how thought can be controlled; or how a powerful mind can be used to discover the secrets of nature; all can be gleaned from his writings and by reading between the lines.

Yoga sutras are not an easy read. They are precise and crisp. India has had a long tradition of passing knowledge from guru to disciple through oral transmission. It can be concluded that the initial exposition by Patanjali must have been very detailed since the subject matter was difficult. With time the subsequent commentators made them concise since it helped in memorizing the sutras. In this process it is quite possible that some important information may have been lost.

Another possibility is that when people did not understand the science behind these sutras some important sutras may have been omitted. Thus, one needs to read between the lines with deep knowledge of modern science to fully appreciate their message. I will try to explain this in detail in sections below.

Yoga Sutras of Patanjali: The Book

The book is divided into four sections with a total of 196 sutras [7]. The sections are *Samadhi Pada* (Section I containing 51 sutras); *Sadhana Pada* (Section II having 55 sutras); *Vibhuti Pada* (Section III having 56 sutras) and the last section called *Kaivalya Pada* (Section IV has 34 sutras).

The first two sections (*Samadhi* and *Sadhana*) talk about how to make the mind and body powerful enough so that one can focus on a single thought for a long time. This focus then leads to *Sanyam* (Patanjali defines it as combination of focus, contemplation, and *Samadhi*). The state of *Samadhi* is reached when the object of focus vanishes, and one gets immersed in its essence. *That is essentially spirituality.*

The third section (*Vibhuti Pada*) is the main section of Yoga Sutras where the Science of Yoga is fully developed. In this section Patanjali talks of using *Sanyam* on various parts of the body to get supernatural powers and on different celestial objects to understand the laws of nature and the Universe.

I feel *Vibhuti Pada* is the real essence of his teachings on the conquest of nature via technology. This section has also inspired me to go on the journey of discovering the interplay of spirituality and technology [8].

Since this section is the *meat of sutras*, I have a feeling that through time it has been tinkered by various commentators. Commentators who did not understand the science, either changed some sutras or may have even omitted some of the deep ones and surprisingly quite a number of distinguished commentators including Swami Vivekananda simply glossed over them [9].

In depth reading of *Vibhuti Pada* also reveals that some sutras are missing in this section since there is an abrupt change in the subject matter from one sutra to another and they are arranged in a haphazard manner.

And the last or the fourth section of the book (*Kaivalya Pada*) talks about how using these supernatural powers and understanding the universal laws, a Yogi gains liberation from the cycle of birth and death. One of the most important tenets of Indian philosophical system is the liberation of a soul, atman, etc. from the cycle of birth and death and Patanjali shows very clearly how to achieve it.

It is also interesting to note that there is no reference to God in the Sutras but only of Universal consciousness (7 out of 196 sutras). Patanjali defines this Universal consciousness as an entity called *Ishvara* (section I.23) *which is beyond time.* Interestingly Patanjali identifies this *Ishvara* (section I.27) with the original sound *Pranava*. Modern theories of Big Bang suggest that the first signal after birth of universe was sound which was like a deep hum [10].

Strangely, reading of these Sutras is somehow mandatory for practitioners of Hath Yoga (Yoga exercises) [11]. However, I feel the study of Yoga Sutras has nothing to do with practicing physical Yoga exercises or Hath Yoga. Patanjali only talks about physical exercise and pranayama in about 5-6 sutras out of 196.

Thus, Yoga sutras should be a recommended reading for students of psychology and all physical sciences. It is a remarkable document on how to live a good and emotionally satisfying life and therefore reading should be recommended in any humanities course.

Science in Yoga Sutras

I will now attempt to show the science embedded in some of the sutras. This is based upon my limited understanding of them and is speculative in nature. However, it shows that if we approach each sutra from a scientific point of view then its beauty becomes evident.

In sections III. 53-55 of *Vibhuti Pada* Patanjali says, "By doing *Sanyam* on a single moment and on the sequence of moments, a yogi gets *Vivek* (exalted knowledge) so that he/she can comprehend all objects in the universe simultaneously irrespective of their location and sequence of change". Or in other words, the Mind of God!

And according to John A Wheeler [12] – One of the world's foremost experts on relativity, Einstein's theory of gravitation can be simply stated [13] as "Events and the interval between events build space-time". The geometric nature of space-time gives rise to gravity, tells the mass how to move, and is the basis of Universe and the movement of all heavenly bodies.

Again, in *Vibhuti Pada* (Section III. 31) Patanjali says that by doing *Sanyam* on the hollow of throat, one conquers hunger and thirst. Recently scientists have discovered that by stimulation of Vagus nerve, hunger pangs can be suppressed. Vagus nerve is concentrated near the esophagus tube – close to the hollow of throat [14]. Few years ago U.S. Food and Drug Administration (US FDA) approved a device, which can electrically stimulate the Vagus nerve so that the brain gets the signal that stomach is full [15].

Similarly in Section III. 43 Patanjali says that by doing *Sanyam* on relationship of body and space, a body could be dissolved cellularly (becomes as light as cotton fibers) and transported from one place to another. This results in the conquest of space. Almost all the UFO abductees' experiences of getting their bodies transported from their home to the alien spacecraft via tunneling and cellular transfer through walls and glass windows mirrors this sutra [16].

Interestingly in Section III. 40 of *Vibhuti Pada*, Patanjali talks about how doing *Sanyam* on vital currents of body a Yogi masters the art of floating over water, mud, or thorns without touching them.

Superficially these two Sutras (III. 40 and 43) talk about transporting of body through space or antigravity process. Yet there is a difference.

It can be conjectured that Patanjali may be alluding that floating over water, etc. could be done via magnetic levitation while Section III. 43 talks about tunneling and intergalactic space travel. Again the experiences of UFO abductees have shown how aliens floated over land and other surfaces [17].

This magnetic levitation could be possible if by some mechanism we can make the body a room temperature superconductor so that it could be levitated magnetically in the Earth's magnetic field. Presently the world does not have this technology.

In another sutra (Section III.21) Patanjali says that doing *Sanyam* on body shape and its changes so that the reflected light does not reach the eyes of beholder one can make the body invisible. This process is used in stealth aircraft where sharp angles and absorption of visible spectrum by the aircraft body makes it invisible [18].

And in Section III. 35 of *Vibhuti Pada* Patanjali talks about how doing *Sanyam* on heart gives complete knowledge of consciousness. Recent scientific discoveries have shown a close connection between the heart and mind [19].

Similarly, he talks about how a Yogi can read the other person's mind by doing *Sanyam* on his *thought structure* and control it (Sutra III. 19). This is being slowly perfected through various processes of Artificial Intelligence (AI) and hypnosis [20].

And in another sutra in *Kaivalya Pada* (Section IV. 1) Patanjali talks about how all the supernatural powers can come to a Yogi by taking drugs! Recent studies on the effect of recreational and mind-altering drugs like LSD etc. have shown enhanced spiritual experiences for drug takers and for some the experience of entity visitations [21]. To my mind this discussion on mind altering drugs in yoga sutras is the first such anywhere in any ancient spiritual text.

In all these Sutras in *Vibhuti Pada* it becomes clear that Patanjali had the detailed knowledge and inner workings of human body. It is quite possible that he might have believed that the human body, which is a greatest piece of machinery and engineering in the universe, was capable of producing supernatural powers.

I therefore feel that if we fully understand the working of the human body then it may be possible to achieve all the supernatural powers that Patanjali talks about.

It can also be conjectured that since the template of human body is of the same time frame as the universe, it is quite possible that it contains almost all the design and attributes of all the technologies we have produced and can think of even in future – including galactic travel.

Also, in *Kaivalya Pada* (sections IV. 2, 3 and 9) Patanjali talks about rebirth happening by chance and not because of past *karma. This is a major departure from accepted notion that your birth is dictated by past karma.*

Even some sutras in *Samadhi* and *Sadhana Pada* (Sections I and II respectively), where Patanjali details the mechanism of thought control and *Sanyam,* are examined through the lens of modern-day neuroscience and brain research then the gems of his teachings become even brighter.

Thus his sutras on memory formation and removal (Patanjali calls memory as *Sanskaras*) and the nature of human thought tallies closely with what we know today about the production and nature of human thought [22].

Similarly, there are other sutras whose knowledge seems to be vindicated by the modern science. I think a whole book can be written about their relevance to modern science and technology. So, there is a need to study *Vibhuti pada* more thoroughly since many secrets in it still need to be rediscovered.

The comparison of Patanjali sutras with modern science is neither to glorify our ancient tradition nor to belittle the latter – both are important in their own way; but to show that all great knowledge originates from the same knowledge space irrespective of the person and the time of its discovery [23].

Also, this comparison helps establish the value and authenticity of the scientific aspect of sutras and gives credence to the fact that other sutras may hold secrets which could be revealed if studied thoroughly. This revelation may perhaps show the path to new understanding of natural laws and novel inventions and *is the main reason why we are trying to read between the lines in these ancient texts.*

Was Sage Patanjali an Extra-terrestrial Astronaut?

All the supernatural powers described in *Vibhuti Pada* have uncanny resemblance with those exhibited by aliens and hence one can speculate that probably Patanjali was also an alien! [24]

In the seminal book on extraterrestrial abductions [25] of humans by UFO inhabitants, John Mack [26] a former Professor of Harvard University had shown that all the persons abducted and taken inside the spaceships (abductees) talked about extraterrestrials floating in air, could interact telepathically with them, could read their minds and modify their thoughts, become invisible and exhibited almost all the powers written in *Vibhuti Pada*. Similar reporting of abductees experiences was also done by Coral and Jim Lorenzen in their book "Encounters with UFO occupants" [27].

This similarity between powers written in Yoga Sutras and exhibited by extraterrestrials is so uncanny that I sometimes think that Sage Patanjali could have been an extraterrestrial being who came to earth almost 2500-3000 years ago to give us this knowledge!

In fact, Patanjali alludes to extraterrestrials in *Vibhuti Pada* (section III. 52) when he says that a Yogi when approached by celestial beings should neither be surprised nor get attached to them because they are hindrance to his salvation. Interestingly this sutra is at the end of *Vibhuti Pada* so that Yogi is supposed to have acquired nearly all the powers attributed to extraterrestrials. Thus he/she can interact as equals with them and ward off their influence rather than being overwhelmed by their powers as most abductees have described [28].

Thus if we understand how a Yogi can get these supernatural powers and understands space-time and Universe then it may show us a possible way to understand mind-matter interaction and probably pave the way for developing galactic travel technologies [29].

Unidentified Flying Objects (UFOs) are real. There have been innumerable sightings and visits by extraterrestrials throughout the history of mankind. In Indian scriptures like Ramayana and Mahabharat there are quite a few descriptions of various gods visiting earth in their flying machines. And recently US government has officially released video clippings of few of these sightings [30]. Similarly, a recent series of Netflix documentaries [31] has further shown the possibilities of these visitations and mankind's quest for understanding the technologies of UFO propulsion.

Propulsion technology used by UFOs effortlessly overcomes earth's gravitational pull and understanding it may help us produce unlimited renewable energies on this planet for our needs and benefits. Hence it is necessary that we invest money and resources in discovering and understanding them.

I firmly believe that the future of mankind is to become a galactic travelling civilization and mastering of the technology to do so can only come when we develop the wisdom through spirituality to use it wisely [32].

Patanjali and Stars

Another tantalizing indication of why Patanjali was an astronaut comes from the fact that in three short sutras he talks about stars! One can ask that in the book about mind control and Yoga what is the relevance of knowledge of stars? Obviously, Patanjali showed that we are what we think. Once the power of comprehension is mastered by the control of thought, then all the knowledge of the world becomes easy to understand. Besides, knowledge of stars was necessary for intergalactic space travel.

Patanjali could have left it at that, but he went on to explain about the knowledge of space and time, and it included stars. He explained that this knowledge could be obtained by understanding Sun, moon, and polar stars. I also think there must have been more sutras about other celestial objects, but they are missing from the book.

In *Vibhuti Pada* (Section III. 27), Patanjali has written that doing *Sanyam* on sun one obtains knowledge of Universe, celestial spaces, or Akash!

This is an interesting concept since focus on Akash or celestial space is far removed from the life-giving rays of the sun which come in various frequencies. Besides, the sun also emits other cosmic rays and particles.

Maybe Patanjali conjectured that the knowledge of sun and how it produces energy may tell us everything about atomic energy, plasma physics, gravity, and other deep science and hence the focus on Universe in this sutra.

It can also be conjectured that he may have meant space-time continuum or gravity since what pervades in all space is gravity and if *Sanyam* is done on the sun, the greatest gravity source in our solar system, then we may understand space-time continuum or the nature of gravity. This is also detailed in Sutras III. 53-55.

He also talks about Moon (Section III. 28) and says that by doing *Sanyam* on moon a Yogi gets knowledge of the arrangement of planets. Newton discovered gravity by thinking about how moon goes around the earth and the falling apple from the tree gave him the idea of gravity and about the motion of planets.

Similarly, Patanjali talks about Pole star (Section III. 29) and says that *Sanyam* on it will help a Yogi understand the movement of all stars and planets. Pole stars through ages have been used not only for navigation on this planet earth but also to map the skies.

It is remarkable that in three short Sutras Patanjali talks about Universe or celestial space and movement of planets and this was much before the time of Copernicus, Plato, Socrates, and Newton.

Major omission in Yoga Sutras

One of the glaring omissions in Yoga Sutras is that there is no mention about Kundalini Yoga [33].

Kundalini yoga is an important part of Tantric yoga system [34] where yogis believe that through the extremely small central canal (called *Shushma Nadi*) of spinal cord, sexual chemicals from its base can be raised to reach the brain where they enhance the communication of neural pathways so that all the parts of brain work in unison and one can attain Samadhi. This is similar to what takes place in the brain during the LSD episode, though the user taking the drug has no control over his/her experience [35].

Yogis also believe that sexual energy is coiled at the base of the spine hence the name *Kundalini* (coiled energy, snake etc.). They believe it can be raised in the central canal – also called *Shushma Nadi*, by will [36].

It seems little strange that Sage Patanjali, who was the first to enunciate the Yoga principles of thought control and mind enhancement, would not have included the science of Kundalini Yoga in it. There could be two reasons for such an omission.

First could be that Patanjali did not believe in Kundalini Yoga as a real physical phenomenon [37]. And the other speculation could be that probably that section could have been extracted by some commentators from his sutras and made into a separate Science of Tantric Yoga. After all the whole of *Vibhuti Pada* is Tantra (technique) of getting supernatural powers and description of Kundalini Yoga would have been very appropriate in it.

My teacher Sage Patanjali

I have been greatly inspired by Patanjali sutras and have felt his spirit has guided me in my quest of spirituality. Hence, I would like to briefly write about my teacher.

Obviously, I never met or knew Patanjali but know him through his Yoga Sutras. Just like Eklavya [38] who learnt his archery by practicing in front of the statue of Dronacharya, I have learnt about the science of Yoga by imagining that the spirit of Patanjali is guiding me.

A great teacher is one who allows his disciple to go through the rough and tumble of learning process, but his guiding hand is always available to show the correct path. So many times when I have been in doubt, I have repeatedly gone to Patanjali's Yoga sutras and discovered the hidden gems [39]. I guess all great books are teachers in this sense.

I came to know about Patanjali at the age of 14 when I read his Yoga Sutras [40] in a book (I. K. Taimni, Science of Yoga) borrowed from a public library in Lucknow [41]. Yoga Sutras is a very difficult book to read and more so since most of the commentators have explained the great science of thought and mind control in an extremely confusing way. Since most of them had no knowledge of science of mind control, their explanations were all clothed in mythology.

A great teacher sometimes has the maximum impact when the student is very sharp. A disciple elicits information from the teacher depending upon his/her intelligence. A great teacher therefore is like an ocean of knowledge, but you can only take that amount of knowledge depending upon the size of your container (brain power).

At age 14 when I was first introduced to my teacher, I could hardly understand what he meant but understood that by following his teachings one could get superhuman powers like flying, omniscience, mind reading and energy of thunderbolt for one's body, among others. Which 14-year-old does not want such powers?

I then got sidetracked by my technology education in IIT Kanpur [42], but his teachings must have remained at the back of my mind, and they exerted an invisible pull so when the time was ripe, I again went back to him for knowledge.

Since then, every time I have doubts about some aspects of science of mind I have gone to Patanjali's Sutras and have discovered new gems. With time my container has also expanded little bit and thus I can absorb more of his knowledge!

Thus, what I have shown in this article is the tip of iceberg as regards the wisdom and genius of Sage Patanjali. What is needed further is to trace the history and origins of his Sutras so that their comprehensive system is established and to study them in depth through the lens of modern science and technology.

Suggested Readings (Books)

1. B. K. S. Iyengar. *Light on the Yoga Sutras of Patanjali.* Harper Collins, India. 1993.

2. I. K. Taimni. *The Science of Yoga : The Yoga Sutras of Patanjali.* Theosophical Publishing House, Adyar, Madras. 1961.

3. David Gordon White *The Yoga Sutra of Patanjali—A Biography.* Princeton University Press, N. J. 2014.

4. Swami Sivananda. *Kundalini Yoga.* Divine Life Society, India. 1994.

5. Swami Vivekananda. *Raja Yoga (Part I and II).* Celephaïs Press, U.K. 2003.

6. Anil K. Rajvanshi. *Exploring the Mind of God – How Technology Guided by Spirituality can lead to Happiness.* Story Mirror, Mumbai. 2022.

7. John E. Mach. *Abduction : Human Encounters with Aliens.* Scribner. 2007.

8. Carol and Jim Lorenzen. *Encounters with UFO Occupants.* Berkley Publishing Corporation. 1976.

9. George Adamski and Desmond Leslie. *Flying Saucers Have Landed.* T. Werner Laurie Ltd., U.K. 1953.

10. John E. Mach. *Passport to Cosmos : Human Transformation and Alien Encounters.* White Crow Books. 2010.

11. Anil K. Rajvanshi. *Nature of Human Thought (Second edition)*. Nimbkar Agricultural Research Institute. 2010.

12. John A. Wheeler. *A Journey into Gravity and Space-Time*. Scientific American Library. 1990.

This chapter was originally published as an essay https://nariphaltan.org/sutrascience.pdf

What is Thought?
Physical and Neurobiological Basis of its Production, Transmission and Interaction with Matter

Introduction

As we discussed in Section I, Patanjali Yoga Sutras is one of the most scientific ancient texts on the working of mind and how to utilize the powerful brain to achieve supernatural powers. However, Patanjali never discussed how thought is produced in the brain or where the memory resides in it.

This section deals with the origin of thought; memory formation; its transmission and interaction with matter. Only when one goes deeper into the science of brain does one realize that certain scriptures contain descriptions resembling the present understanding of brain.

It follows our thesis that the commentators of lots of scriptures did not know the science and hence could never interpret the true meaning of the sutras.

A deep analysis of this theme section has been done by AI (Gemini Deep Search). Readers may find the analysis and review interesting [1].

This chapter was published as an e-essay, and I have put it in the book in its original form for completeness. It is divided into the following sections:

Preface

Section A: Thought

Section B: Memory Production and Removal

Section C: Thought Transmission

Section D: Interaction with Matter

Preface

In 2004 I wrote my first book entitled "Nature of Human Thought". In it and in a subsequent edition I tried to cover some ideas on how thought is formed and transmitted [2]. The ideas were speculative in nature, but I tried my best, with the knowledge available at that time, to explain the mechanism of how thought could be formed in the brain and transmitted. The basic framework was explained but the details were missing.

Since then, I have thought a little more about the subject and I present in this essay a possible neurobiological and physical mechanism of thought production and memory formation. And furthermore, a possible mechanism for its transmission and interaction with matter and gravity. I also speculate on the unexplored possibilities which might provide a detailed mathematical foundation of the nature of individual thought.

I have been exploring and writing about these issues since 1977 though the desire to understand them started from my childhood when I started practicing spirituality in earnest [3]. These ideas since 1977 were initially written down in a diary form [4] and then distilled in my first book, "Nature of Human Thought" [5] which was published in 2004 and its second edition in 2010.

Recently I have written another book "Exploring the Mind of God – How Technology Guided by Spirituality Can Lead to Happiness" which extends and explores mind-matter interaction issues further [6]. Again, the details were missing and so in this essay I have tried to explain them based on existing physical laws.

Most of the times scientists scoff at these conjectural ideas and term them pseudo-science. However if in early 1800s somebody had told mankind about Einstein's theory of relativity and the space-time continuum [7], people would have had the same reaction as today's so called hard-core scientists have about mind-matter subjects. *The black magic of today is often the science of tomorrow!*

The spirit of science encourages us to conjecture and our imagination to flower and the only validity of such conjectures is the proof from experiments. It is my firm belief that we should have an open mind about mind-matter interaction and try to figure out how it could be possible. This essay is therefore for those readers who have an open mind about such possibilities.

Structure of the essay

The essay is divided into four sections. The first section deals with thought production. A very novel concept of thought as a hologram, based on biophotons production in the synaptic cleft, has been introduced and developed.

The second section talks about the nature of memory; its production; its possible location in the brain and outside it; and a possible mechanism of its removal.

The third section talks about how thought can be transmitted from the brain and what laws could make it happen. Connected with this is the process of knowledge perception where the novel concept of quantum entanglement is used to describe it.

And the last section is about how human thought could interact with matter and gravity. In the ultimate analysis this interaction with gravity may allow us eventually to get out of the gravity field. Some speculative ideas on how it may happen, based on the concept of deep thought as a soliton, are explored in this section.

I have been working on this subject of "What is Thought" on-and-off for the last 50 years. The trigger was a sudden idea that came to me out of the blue in 1977 that human thought and gravity are related [8]. This happened in Gainesville, Florida when I was deeply involved in my Ph.D. work [9] on solar energy and the idea of gravity was as far removed from my mind as earth from the sun!

Yet this sudden and unexpected idea was so powerful that it caught hold of my mind for next 4-5 months and I could hardly concentrate on anything else. Since this idea came so suddenly and powerfully, I was convinced that it was true – otherwise it would not have come.

In 1981 I came back to India to work on rural development in our small NGO – Nimbkar Agricultural Research Institute [10]. I therefore could only take up seriously the matter of spirituality and understanding of human thought in early 2000.

I am always reminded of Einstein's words of wisdom where he said that for somebody to do deep thinking on any issue, he should lock himself in a lighthouse! With no distractions the focus is achieved.

My small Institute is my lighthouse, and I feel very blessed and grateful to higher powers who have guided me and allowed me to focus on this and other deep issues and whatever little truth I have been able to glean has given me great joy and happiness.

The major source of inspiration for writing this essay has been Patanjali Yoga Sutras [11]. I have been guided by the spirit of sage Patanjali in the areas of human thought and mind-matter interaction. The more I study his sutras the more I realize the ocean of knowledge in his writings.

This essay was published as an e-booklet and is freely available on the net for wider circulation. https://nariphaltan.org/whatisthought.pdf [12].

Section A: Thought

Introduction

Almost all of us, sometime or the other in our life, have gone through the experience of feeling that somebody is following or watching us. Whether it is a human being or an animal it makes us turn our neck to see what it is and investigate. Similarly, there have been innumerable instances where people and animals have sensed danger before it strikes them [13]. What is the nature of the signal that tells our mind that somebody is watching us intently or there is a lurking danger and how is that signal generated and sent from the pursuer's brain? In other words what is thought and how is it generated and transmitted?

Since time immemorial mankind has thought, discussed and written about the origin of human thought. Religious writings are basically a discussion on them. Perhaps the greatest treatise on it has been Patanjali's Yoga Sutras, [14] which to my mind is still one of the most definitive and scientific writings on the control of human thought.

Patanjali's book is the oldest book on Yoga. It is believed that he wrote his book some time in 300 BC or even earlier though there is still dispute about the date. Patanjali defines Yoga as control of thought waves. This is probably the first definition of Yoga. He then describes how through Yoga, one can produce concentration and how this concentrated thought can be used to gain physical and spiritual powers for a person's ultimate enlightenment [15].

Interestingly sage Patanjali does not address the central question of how and where the thought originates in the brain but gives details on how to control it for achieving mastery over natural forces. In this essay we will make use of recent developments in brain research to understand thought, mind and consciousness.

Generally human thought has been considered by philosophers, religious leaders etc. as non-material in nature. However, a result (thought) produced by a physical brain must be physical in nature and should be governed by physical laws. I will attempt to throw light on what these laws could be. Most of the concepts presented here are intuitive in nature with very little mathematical formulation.

Scientists have conducted many studies all over the world to find out how the brain works. Magnetic resonance imaging (MRI) techniques, which are non-invasive in nature, are normally used in mapping the brain. Recently scientists have started using functional MRI (fMRI) for sharper images [16]. Thus, fMRI scans are taken of the brain under different stimuli which show up on the computer screen as maps of blood flow in the brain. Scientists say that the place of maximum blood flow is the area where thought of a particular nature is generated. Yet no mechanism has been put forward on how thought is produced.

Human Thought Production

It is an accepted fact that a thought is produced when brain neurons fire. There are close to 80-100 billion neurons in the brain (the exact figure is not known) [17]. For a simple thought like what is the colour of a flower, form of a cat or a dog, etc. we can conjecture that a small portion of the neurons fire but in deep concentration leading to *Samadhi* [18] via the process of *Sanyam* [19] (combination of concentration and contemplation on a single subject or an object for a long time) almost all the neurons fire to produce a deep thought. Thus, the difference between deep and shallow thought is its intensity and duration.

When neurons fire, they communicate with each other by forming neural pathways. Activation of neural pathways in turn triggers firing of neurons. This activation is triggered either by signals from sense organs or stimulation of certain memory space in the brain. Firing of neurons therefore helps them to communicate with each other.

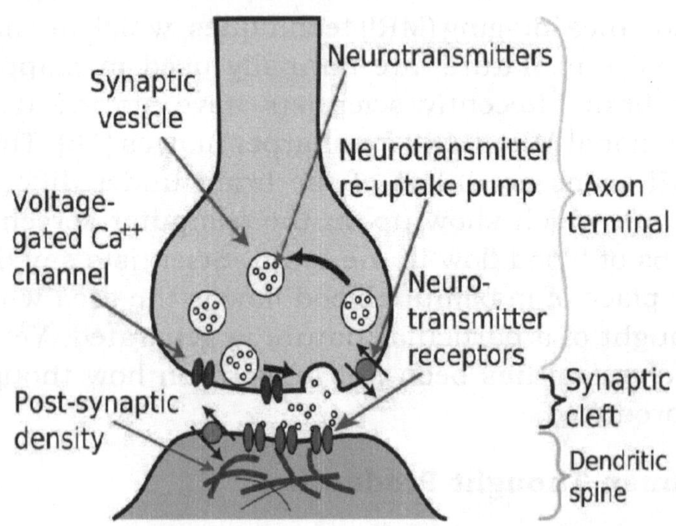

During this communication electrical signal from a neuron is converted into chemicals (neurotransmitters)[20] and transmitted across the synaptic cleft to another neuron where it is again converted to electrical signal for the onward journey.

Synaptic cleft [21] is a tiny space of about 20 nanometers (nm) between an axon and a dendrite and is the place where two neurons exchange information via neurotransmitters (NT).

A neuron has three parts. At one end is dendrite which accepts NT from other neurons; the central nucleus which is the heart of neuron and a long nerve fiber called axon whose end (synapse) releases the NT for transmitting to another neuron. *A large number of neurons connected like this forms a neural pathway.*

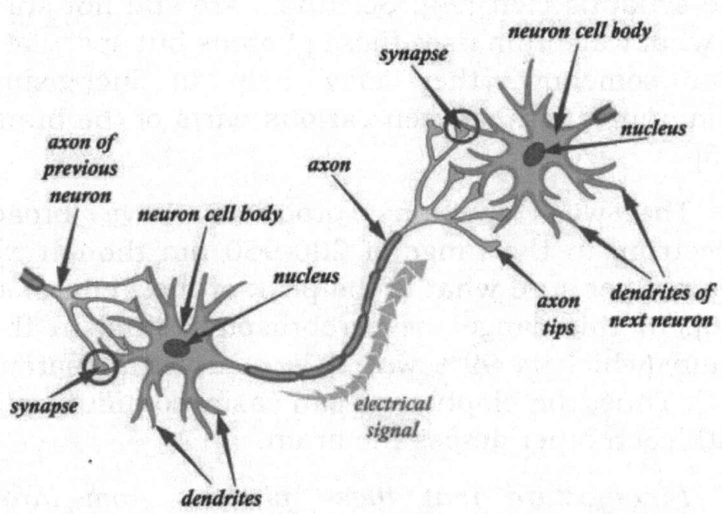

Why did nature produce this type of diode-based [22] communication system where the electrical signal from the neuron, which goes in one direction, is first converted into chemicals (neurotransmitters), and transmitted through synaptic cleft and again converted back into the electrical signal in the next neuron?

A possible answer could be that during this conversion in synaptic cleft, weak biophotons are produced which are the genesis of thought. Anytime a chemical reaction takes place (production of NTs and their acceptance in NT receptors are such reactions) it produces weak photons [23]. *This is the nature of the chemical bond.*

Weak photon production was experimentally observed in the brain in the late 2010s when scientists detected them being emitted during the firing of the neurons and transfer of neurotransmitters across the synaptic cleft [24]. Scientists are still not sure in what way brain uses these photons but speculate that somehow, they may help in increasing communication between various parts of the brain [25].

The weak photons produced have broad spectrum in the range of 200-950 nm though we are not yet sure what is the peak of their emission [26]. In this range the cerebrospinal fluid in the brain (which is 99% water) is nearly transparent [27]. Thus, the biophotons can easily communicate with each other across the brain.

I conjecture that these photons from large number of neural pathways synchronize via a non-linear process to form a three-dimensional hologram [28] *which we can call a thought. Hence the origin of thought probably occurs in large number of synaptic clefts!*

Photon production at synaptic cleft is further cemented by another piece of evidence. Research suggests sleep helps in flushing out toxic protein waste and other biological debris from the brain [29]. These toxins are produced in the synaptic cleft during the waking hours. Research has also shown that in sleep the connections *between neurons are slightly loosened and this helps in opening up the channels* through which the debris flows into the blood stream [30].

With sleep deprivation the toxin load builds up in the cleft creating diminished and distorted photon production. This results in dysfunction of thought formation process, leading to judgment impairment, mental illnesses like depression, heart problems, obesity, and drastic reduction in general well-being of an individual.

Brain Complexity and Synchronization of Thought Photons

How do photons from millions of synapses synchronize and form a coherent thought? For that we will have to examine the brain complexity, understand large number mathematics and possible synchronization mechanism.

Just to give a sense of complexity of the brain let us look at the numbers of possible neural pathways in the brain. There are close to 80-100 billion neurons in the brain. Each neuron has many dendrites and axons which connect it to other neurons. Recent scientific evidence also suggests that besides neurons another type of cells called glial cells also take part in communication [31].

Glial cells outnumber neurons by nine to one and can modify the signals transmitted by each neuron. There are therefore guestimates that 10^{15} synapses in the brain maybe involved in communication [32]. Thus, the number of different combinations for neural pathways and thought production are mind-boggling. That is the reason why the human mind can generate millions and zillions of thoughts!

However, the photons from each synapse must be synchronized with others to produce a stable thought structure. This synchronization takes place via the positive feedback type mechanism so that each photon is influenced by others and is guided by an entity called 'I' (ego, will, sense of identity, etc.) [33]. This is similar to the mechanism where fireflies in large numbers synchronize their firing [34]. I conjecture that this type of synchronization might produce a thought hologram.

Ego acts like a symphony director [35] and helps provide the necessary energy and focus to maintain a given thought for a certain time. It also constantly compares it with signals from outside (those we receive through our senses) to give us a sense of reality.

We still do not completely understand how ego, or 'I' [36] can influence this process, but just like the music conductor who determines which part of the orchestra plays for how long, 'I' decides how long a particular thought will remain in the "vision" field. *This process is called concentration and seems to also exist in other animals.*

With practice, concentration becomes strong till a person can make nearly all the 80-100 billion neurons fire in a laser-like fashion for a long time on a single thought. This is the genesis of meditation or *Samadhi* [37] and is the outcome of *Sanyam* [38]. According to Sage Patanjali *Sanyam*, done on any subject results in its complete knowledge. Thus, deep concentration is the basis by which all great discoveries in science, art, and any other human endeavor are made [39].

This deep thought produced continuously also helps dissolve memory knots of the brain since this activity requires increased number of neural pathways and hence the loosening of existing memories. We will discuss this in detail in the next section (section B).

Patanjali says that removing memory knots or *sanskars* makes the mind like a crystal so that any object or subject occupies the whole brain [40]. Or in other words when memory knots are resolved the processing power of the brain increases exponentially and allows the brain to focus on a single object or subject in a laser-like manner. Hence the reference to crystal-like clarity of the brain.

The production of weak photons for thought formation could also be the reason why many Yogis have experienced seeing white light during intense meditation [41]. Similarly the observation of white light by persons during near death experience (NDE) [42] could be an outcome of nearly all the brain neurons firing during the final exit.

Unexplored Possibilities

Here are some of the unexplored and speculative possibilities which can give mathematical formulation for thought production.

1. We still do not know how many Neurotransmitters (NTs) are released per firing of neuron [43].

2. There are speculations that it is anywhere between 2 and 20 [44].

3. Also, the molecular structure of each NT and receptor is not fully understood.

4. Besides how many of these NTs are captured by receptors of the next neuron is also not known [45].

5. The problem is compounded by the fact that we do not have the technology to see real time happenings in the synapse [46].

6. If we can find the number of NTs released and their capture by receptors then the energy and frequency of biophotons can be calculated and a possible hologram could be created from this data.

7. That will be the first attempt to calculate the structure of a single thought!

Section B: Memory Production and Removal

Introduction

We are defined by our memories. They are the only things we can call our own. All our experiences, ego, I, and our existence are the sum and substance of our lifetime memories. They guide us on our future journey in life and till the end of our existence those memories are with us.

Most of our memories can be divided into pleasant and unpleasant ones. These memories give rise to a whole range of emotions – love, hatred, jealousy, fear, happiness etc. To live a good and happy life we should strive to have mostly pleasant memories and see how the unpleasant ones can be reduced or removed. One of the main tenets of Indian *Yogic* system is complete removal of our memories at the time of death or final exit so that we are liberated from the cycle of birth and death [47].

But what are memories; and where in the brain do they reside? Also how are they formed; and what is the possible mechanism of their removal? We will try to explore and explain these issues based on the material presented in Section A.

Previous Research

Memory, its origin, and spatial location in the brain has been researched for hundreds of years. Extensive literature on it exists and hence this article is not a place to write the history of memory research, but we will briefly touch the salient features of previous research. One of the seminal works on memory was done by Eric Kandel who got the 2000 Nobel Prize for his work on this subject [48]. Kandel's main discovery was that synapse plays an important role in memory formation and the consolidation of memory changes the synapse itself. This pioneering work on neurobiological basis of memory showed the process of memory formation and consolidation in few neurons but it did not show where the memory is located and how it is related to consciousness [49].

At the same time the existing theories on neurological basis of memory formation also do not explain the pliability and plasticity of neurons and neural networks. Scientists have recently found that with time the original neural networks shift spatially and yet are able to retain the same memory [50]. How this happens is still a mystery and thus we do not know where the memory exists and exactly what it is.

Memory Formation

As we saw in Section A each thought is the result of activation of a unique set of neural pathways though we still do not know the number of neural pathways needed for its production. *In fact, the formation of such unique neural pathways is the memory. So, activation of neural pathways results in memory recall and neurons firing in these pathways produce a thought.* With practice and constant flow of communication (both chemical and electrical) through these neural pathways, memory of that particular object gets strengthened.

Neural pathways are made the moment brain starts forming in the womb. Very rudimentary memory of movement, swallowing, etc. starts in the second and third trimester of pregnancy. Prenatal memory starts forming around 30 weeks after conception [51]. After this time, the fetus is affected by the food the mother consumes. A fair amount of good data exists on how alcohol and drug use by mothers at this stage affect the children later in life.

The moment a child is born there is an explosion in memory formation. A child's brain is like a sponge for information intake since neural pathways must be established. So, the ears, nose and other sensory organs start sending signals to the brain for the formation of neural pathways.

Nevertheless, I feel that the basic memory which exists in every life form at the time of birth is the preservation of its form [52]. How this memory is inbuilt in genetic code is still a mystery. This form-preservation memory gives rise to emotions like fear and the desire to procreate – both basic instincts to preserve the form. Both these memories are eternal to life and part of evolutionary process.

However, the first solid memories are those when eyes start focusing. The input signals from the eyes are coordinated with those from the ears and help establish and stimulate the neural pathways which results in the formation of a random thought hologram. *This hologram is compared with the actual object and, when after many comparisons the exact match takes place, then the memory is etched in the brain.*

The "comparer" of reality and hologram in this case is the nascent ego of the child which is still developing but is not strong enough to focus on a particular thing for a long time. This results in memories being formed and forgotten. Though the brain at this age is like a sponge for absorbing information, the lack of focus does not allow the memories to become strong.

This is the reason why children have very few memories till the age of 2-3 years. With the developing of ego as we age, longer focus results and hence a stronger memory [53]. The memory is further strengthened when the child repeatedly performs the process of seeing, validating, and memorizing. This also helps in making neural pathways stronger when the child repeatedly produces the thought hologram of a given object.

Children are therefore particularly good at doing mundane things repeatedly because this is how they set up and consolidate their memories. Since the brain is like a sponge in childhood, those repeated early neural pathways are strong and thus some of the childhood memories (after the age of 3-4 years) are very powerful.

Many times, the parents get exasperated with a child repeatedly performing these mundane actions and scold the child. This should not be done because scolding creates fear-complex memories, and the new learning is retarded.

As we grow older this process of memory formation and consolidation is repeated and a whole network of neural pathways is formed. The sum and substance of our experiences and memories give rise to our sense of self and is the genesis of ego [54]. If the memory is not strengthened by repeated experiences, then those neural pathways are used for something else and hence the memory becomes weak and maybe lost as happens in children till the age of 2-3 years.

Therefore chanting, rote learning and associating the images with signposts, etc. are ways of strengthening the memory. Nevertheless, there are some people who possess photographic memory. They can immediately remember most of the details the moment they become aware of something. This happens because their brain possesses superior processing power which is mostly inborn and may have a genetic element to it.

Our memory formation is based on a sequence of events received through our senses and hence the time is embedded in the memories. They are replayed as a movie and thus the sequence of events tells us about the passage of time. This is the genesis of time perception [55].

Since the neural pathways are formed sequentially, hence during recall one set of neural pathways triggers another set. It is therefore quite possible that the *neural pathways of such events reside close to each other in the brain otherwise sequencing may be difficult.*

This triggering of sets of neural pathways is probably facilitated by the ego [56]. When ego becomes weak the triggering is reduced, and the sequencing is lost. This happens temporarily during dreaming; and permanently in dementia, Alzheimer's disease, and other brain maladies [57].

The proximity of neural pathways may also explain why one type of thought triggers other thoughts of similar nature! Thus, both dark and pleasant thoughts come in bunches.

Memory Removal

In everybody's life there are both painful and happy memories. It will be wonderful if somehow, we can get the ability to reduce or remove those painful memories. Then we can have a better and happier life. Most people think that if we do not think about the painful memories then they are gone. But painful memories produce strong psychological knots which remain buried in the brain. When by some trigger they get reactivated, the pain comes back again. To remove the pain a mechanism of actively removing such memories is necessary.

A possible mechanism of memory removal is to focus on a single thought for an exceptionally long time. It is called *Sanyam* in *Patanjali Yoga Sutras* [58]. Production of *Sanyam* requires large number of neural pathways since huge processing power is needed. This may help in the removal of the other memories since those neural pathways are used for this particular thought. With discipline, willpower, and passage of time the brain can become very pliable so that *Sanyam* results effortlessly.

As Patanjali says in his *yoga sutras*; *"When a brain becomes powerful and nimble it is like a pure crystal which takes the color and shape of the object which comes in its view"* [59]. Such a brain is therefore able to focus like a laser on anything that occupies its vision field.

This process has also been corroborated by recent work in memory formation where scientists have shown that by thinking deeply on certain object the synapses are weakened for a short time [60]. They can then be modified to form pathways for other memories. This plasticity of memory is one reason why sometimes in extreme circumstances of brain surgery and removal of some parts of the brain, it can still allow a patient to work and form new neural pathways and hence memories [61].

Memory removal is the most important aspect of Indian *Yogic* system which asserts that this leads to liberation from the cycle of death and rebirth. Also, with less memory attached to our soul during the final exit, we can tunnel through the drag of gravity and other souls and reach the other worlds [62]. *This is the easiest way to get out of the earth's gravity field!*

Memory removal also helps in unraveling memory knots, mostly made of emotional incidents, and helps in resolving emotional conflicts. There are many instances where the resolution of such conflicts helped people to die peacefully [63]. Another way to remove unpleasant memories is to cultivate the habit of continuously thinking about the pleasant incidences [64] that have happened in our lives. It is a difficult process but practised regularly could help in resolving unhappy memories.

Many times, it happens that our PC's, laptops, and other computing devices become slow since they are cluttered with folders and other materials which take up the working memory space. After downloading most of the information on an external hard disk, the memory of the PC is restored, and it functions faster and smoothly. In the same way uncluttering of the brain (by removing the psychological memory knots) will allow it to function properly and faster.

Nevertheless, there are other powerful and intense memories which are the result of emotional and painful episodes. These episodes, when they occur, result in occupying the whole brain so that the focus of the brain is single-pointed. It is almost like *Samadhi.* These memories are very difficult to erase but necessary to be removed for a happy life.

Can Memories Exist Outside the Human Brain?

It is possible that powerful emotional memories can form a very deep thought resulting in a stable soliton and can exist for a long time [65]. I conjecture that such stable memories may reside in Knowledge Space (KS). Knowledge space could be equivalent to external hard disk where our strongest memories get stored automatically.

I define Knowledge space (KS) as a space which may contain information structures or memories which are very stable and will remain there for a very long time [66]. This is similar to cloud storage. However, cloud storage is connected to our devices via cables and processors. Whereas the KS maybe tethered to our gravitational field though this is just a conjecture. How memories can go and reside in KS is speculated and discussed in Section C (transmission of thought).

This knowledge space may also contain fundamental knowledge produced in the past and is continuously fed by the ever-increasing knowledge from various civilizations as earth travels around the Milky Way Galaxy. A prepared and focused human mind can access knowledge from this space, and I feel that great discoveries of mankind have come from such access [67].

There are also indications that strong emotional memories may be attached to inanimate objects. There is a fair amount of data from all over the world [68] where the mediums have been able to access the memories from such objects and it has resulted in new finds of buried ancient structures (almost 15-20,000 years old); ability to tell sequence of events about unnatural deaths; and timelines of civilizations long gone and lost [69].

It seems that the physical objects (like a stone, bone or any other object used by the people long dead) are somehow attached to the memories of those persons in KS and the mediums are able to access them. In scientific language this ability is called "Intuitive Archeology" [70].

Such ability to recall the memories or past events of people by simply touching them was shown by Swami Vivekananda – the Indian spiritual leader [71]. This ability is also mentioned in Patanjali Yoga Darshan; *"By doing Sanyam on other person's mind, a Yogi gets the knowledge of that person's thought waves but not the contents of his mind"* [72].

It is also possible that KS may have templates of various life forms. The memories of life forms remain in KS because these forms existed for an exceedingly long time (couple of million years). Thus, either a deep thought for a long time or "nearly constant" life forms for a long time produce these stable memories in KS. Even if the physical form disintegrates the ghost or memories remain in KS. This memory of forms or templates maybe the basis (besides the regular evolutionary forces) of new life forms for a young life-sustaining planet as it comes across KS in its journey through space [73].

We can also conjecture that the transfer of memories to KS from our brain is via soliton hologram which is a powerful but very stable thought and is like a filter. Thus only deep emotional memories get transferred and mundane memories remain behind in the brain [74]. This process helps to reduce the loading of KS. The mundane memories, however, need to be removed via the memory removal process outlined in the previous section.

Complete Trace Removal

In the modern internet and world wide web if we want to completely remove our trace then firstly, we need to format our PCs and then remove all the information from the net. This is not easy since the deep web contains the archived material with which we have been associated, and it is exceedingly difficult to remove all of it. Thus, somehow and somewhere the past can catch up with us!

In the same way we need to remove memories from the brain and those from KS to get complete liberation from the cycle of birth and death [75]. Just like the hard disk can be formatted or cleaned when it is attached to the PC or a similar device, similarly the cleaning of memories in KS can only be done by intense thinking via the human brain. And as Patanjali says in his *Yoga Sutras, "When the mutations of gunas cease to function, flow of time stops and Kaivalya (Nirvana) results"*. This results in complete removal of trace memories and liberation of yogi.

Otherwise, the traces of our memories in KS can force our rebirth either here on this planet or other planets. This could probably be the genesis of *Karma* concept so often mentioned in Indian philosophy [76].

Section C. Thought Transmission

Introduction

Very often we have felt that when we are thinking deeply about somebody, lo and behold we get news about that person either by a letter, email or phone call. In this regard there is a celebrated case of Hans Berger [77], the inventor of electroencephalogram (EEG). Sometime in 1893 he was seriously hurt during horse riding. His sister, who stayed far away immediately sensed his condition and asked her father to send a telegram inquiring about him. Berger felt this was a clear case of telepathy and it set him thinking about how this could have happened. In the process he developed EEG to measure the brain waves in the hope that they somehow could be transmitted to long distances. Similarly, there have been few cases where some dogs know when their owners are coming home [78].

So, what is the signal that tells us about these things and how is that signal transmitted to long distances - in other words what is telepathy? [79]. Thus, in this section we will talk about how thought can be transmitted from one brain to another.

We have seen how the generation of thought and its validation of the outside world through the signals received from our senses, gives us a sense of reality. Besides, this internal churning in the brain makes us creative and gives us a sense of humanness. When we can resolve some of the memory knots through this internal churning, then it also gives us a sense of well-being and happiness. All these activities require intense concentration.

Nevertheless, a deep thought which is a result of tremendous concentration for a long time is also a leaky thought! It not only helps us evaluate various scenarios but is also automatically transmitted and has an effect on the mind of others who are in the vicinity of a deep thinker. This results in mind-bending experience (or the sense of danger) that some people feel when they are in the presence of such beings. These thoughts can bring in the feelings of either peace and happiness or evil intentions depending upon the personality and mental makeup of the sender.

Presence of a Being

Very often people have felt a sense of well-being and happiness in the vicinity of an enlightened human being. These beings continuously produce a thought of high quality which leaks from their brain and affects anybody who encounters it. Similarly, there are other human beings who are evil and continuously have evil intentions about society and how to harm others. These evil thoughts also affect people and have been the cause of a lot of misery in the world.

Some examples of this powerful brain interaction have been reported by UFO abductees [80]. Most abductees felt very frightened when they encountered alien beings. They felt as if their whole life was sucked out of them and these encounters also wiped out all their memories of the event [81]. Patanjali has alluded to such a process in his Yoga Sutras: *"A Yogi not only can read the mind of others but can also take command of his/her mind and body"* [82].

On terrestrial level, these leaky thoughts from a powerful brain also create an aura, either good or bad, around the person, and is felt by everybody who encounters him/her.

At present this aura and thought cannot be transmitted by any known technological means like phones, video, internet, etc. The day we will be able to project or transmit them to large distances through our technology will be the day when man-machine interface will vanish. *Presently powerful thoughts can only be transmitted by human brains. I conjecture that they can also be transmitted over long distances, and we will explore it in this essay.*

Nevertheless, in order to feel the presence or aura, one's mind should also be sensitive to the feelings. A person devoid of such sensitivity cannot feel a presence. Mind is both a receiver and a broadcaster of strong thoughts and a sensitive mind is able to receive them and feel the presence of the being.

However, a sensitive mind is sometimes a curse because it can be easily distracted by any strong thought it perceives. It therefore requires great willpower to ward off influences from a powerful mind.

We also sometimes hype ourselves into a state of awe in the presence of a well-known personality and do not see the flaws in that person. This hype is, however, sensed by these personalities, and they get an added boost to their energy levels. Besides it also helps them to control their followers. Many orators and public figures have experienced and commented on this.

Nevertheless, a genuine feeling of warmth, love, kindness and humility can only be felt when in the presence of a great soul. Thus, if all of us follow our basic gut feelings and meet such souls then we should be thankful for our luck. Such people's friendship should be cultivated and cherished. I also think this is a good way to judge a person's greatness.

One can create a benevolent "presence" by developing a calm mind. Calmness of mind comes from internal security, which is an outcome of spirituality. A person who is at peace with himself/ herself can radiate a tremendous calmness and help spread it. There have been many instances where people have felt this calmness in the presence of great souls like Mahatma Gandhi [83], Vivekananda [84], etc.

It is not necessary that only so called "god men" or well-known figures have a presence. Quite a number of times one can find such a presence in ordinary people. In fact, many times well-known people are very troubled human beings. Their stakes in power, position or money are very high and higher the stakes are, higher their insecurity is. They therefore frequently radiate this insecurity which tends to be quite unpleasant.

Thought Transmission

So how are these thoughts, aura, and presence radiated outside the brain and become leaky thoughts? Sage Patanjali has alluded to this in his sutras (III.1-4). He says that doing *Sanyam* on anything brings in great knowledge and wisdom [85].

Sanyam is a combination of *Dhyan* (concentration); *Dharan* (keeping it in the vision field of our mind); and *Samadhi* (complete immersion in the object or subject of focus and inquiry). When *Sanyam* is done on anything, Patanjali says, a complete knowledge of the subject is achieved. This has been the basis of all the great discoveries and inventions of the world [86].

Our theory of deep thought hologram and its leaky nature follow this approach. We perceive reality by producing the hologram and validating it with signals from our senses. With concentration, mediated by ego, we try to keep that hologram in the vision field of the brain for a longer time to evaluate the object or subject [87].

With even greater concentration this hologram acts like a laser because of its intensity; becomes leaky and gets transmitted to the outside world. This transmission then allows this hologram to interact with the object or subject of our focus in an induced fit type arrangement and gives back to us the signal whether the information or our inference is correct or wrong! [88].

But how is the signal from the object of focus received by our brain? For objects that we can see and feel it is quite easy because our senses guide us in doing so. But for the concepts and subjects that we do not see and are beyond our reach what is the mechanism? *The science of quantum entanglement may provide a possible answer.*

Knowledge Perception via Quantum Entanglement

Quantum entanglement [89] (Spooky action at a distance as Einstein described it) is a concept which states that photons or even particles created or generated are entangled with each other such that the knowledge of one can describe the other, no matter how far apart they are.

We can conjecture that our concentrated thought hologram that leaks out and interacts with the object or subject of perception somehow changes the property of hologram in the brain via the entanglement process. *This continuous dialogue between these holograms via entanglement brings us the knowledge.*

The increased concentration makes it possible to increase the frequency and intensity of the holograms and it is quite possible that this intense thought behaves like a laser so that attenuation is reduced, and the induced fit type arrangement is established and maintained for considerable amount of time [90].

We also discussed in Section A that thought holograms may have wavelength signature in the near and far infrared range. The human skull [91] and hair [92] are also nearly transparent in this range and hence it is quite possible that intense thought could easily be transmitted out of the brain. Besides hair may also act like an antenna and aid in the thought transmission and reception [93].

Normally a thought inside the brain dissipates rapidly since many new thought holograms are being produced. This results in brain chatter. However, a thought which is produced with intense concentration and for a long time may be transmitted easily as explained. The intensity of this hologram will also decide how far it can go since the $1/r^2$ attenuation (inverse square law) could dilute it rapidly [94].

So how does one produce a thought hologram which remains stable and can travel to long distances? The science of soliton may be able to explain it [95].

Deep Thought Hologram as a Soliton Wave

Soliton is a wave which can remain stable for almost infinite time and can travel to great distances without dissipating [96]. These waves arise *because of the far-from-equilibrium and hence non-linear nature of the wave phenomenon* and have been observed in liquids, gases, optics and even in space. When the conditions are right (non-linearity becomes intense) a critical threshold is achieved and according to Catastrophe Theory soliton structure can be formed [97]. The word soliton is apparently derived from solitary wave which, being stable, acts almost like a particle. Hence soliton rhymes with electron!

Concentrated thought hologram is a three-dimensional, far-from-equilibrium, wave and may follow the soliton laws. *It can therefore be conjectured that a thought hologram which is an outcome of tremendous concentration for a long time can form a soliton* [98].

This thought-hologram soliton may also interact with gravity and matter (details are given in the next section). The ability of this soliton to travel long distances and remain stable could be the basis of clairvoyant powers [99] that some yogis have exhibited and to a limited extent experimentally observed [100]. Anecdotal evidence suggests that Aurobindo Ghosh an Indian spiritual guru had an ability to sense thought packets sent to him [101].

Since thought solitons are very stable structures, it is tempting to think that they may form stable memories and may reside in Knowledge Space [102]. These memories could also be the basis of Karma that is talked about in the Indian Philosophy [103].

Section D. Interaction with Matter

Introduction

Throughout the history of human civilization there have been many instances where so-called "miracles" have been performed. These have included levitation, production of material things from thin air, physical healing, etc. The nature of these miracles is the same, irrespective of religions and different civilizations. Some of their accounts have been exaggerated and found fraudulent but a fair body of data shows remarkable consistency in their nature and reporting though the producers of such miracles always claimed that God or higher forces and entities use them as medium [104].

However, I feel that these *events have taken place because of the interaction of human thought with gravity and material surroundings*. After all, a thought produced by the physical brain must be physical in nature and hence governed by certain scientific laws. Thus, curiosity arose about which laws of science operate to make these things happen. This essay is my humble attempt in trying to understand them.

Why Study Mind-Matter?

Curiosity is one part, but a major reason is that it may lead to a quantum jump in the evolution of mankind.

As I will show in subsequent sections, mind-matter interaction is an obvious consequence of deep thought hologram production and transmission [105]. This deep thought or *Sanyam* [106] according to Patanjali Yoga Sutras helps us get enlightenment, gives us great happiness and joy and leads to liberation from the cycle of birth and death. This is a major step towards the removal of pain.

And the second reason is that mind-matter interaction may provide a mechanism for us to overcome gravity for terrestrial travel. All our travel on this planet is governed by developing machines to overcome gravity. If we develop science and technology to overcome it, then it will tremendously reduce the world's energy burden. We also yearn to get out of the gravitational field of the earth and become an intergalactic travelling civilization. I firmly believe that our origins are extraterrestrial [107] and we long to go back to our roots in distant galaxies and planets. These other worlds were our heavens of mythology.

Thought and Gravity Interaction

As we have discussed in Section C, deep thought soliton can remain stable and travel to long distances. This can only happen when it can interact with space- time matrix. Or in other words, how can thought and gravity be correlated?

According to Albert Einstein gravity is nothing else but a curvature of space-time continuum and hence geometric in nature [108]. *It is my conjecture that since the structure of deep thought soliton is also geometric, it is possible that both gravity and deep thought are related at a deeper level.* This line of thinking is also corroborated by recent theories of gravity which focus on its emergence from holography and photon production [109,110].

Also, according to the general theory of gravitation, light bends around massive bodies [111]. This is because massive bodies distort the space-time matrix and the shortest path for light travel is geodesic [112]. Hence light appears to bend when it passes heavy bodies like sun. This was one of the great triumphs of Einstein's theory of gravitation.

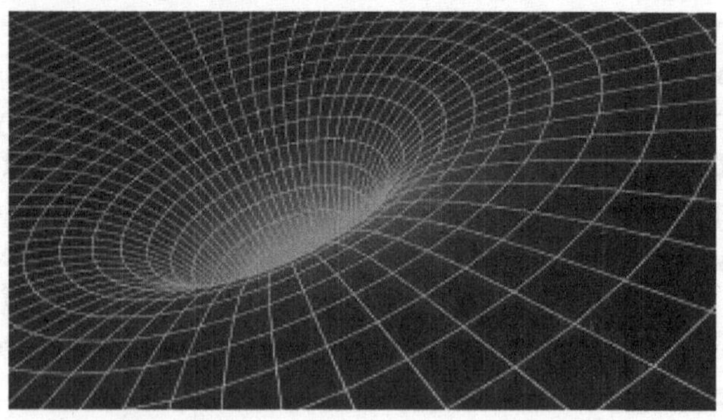

Since gravity bends light [113], we can conjecture by principle of equivalence that light should also bend the space-time matrix! This is the line of thinking we will employ in our quest to find the relationship between deep human thought and gravity.

Gravitation theory also shows that a combination of energy and momentum can curve space-time matrix. Though photons are massless particles, they have energy and momentum – two important attributes for bending space-time matrix. *Hence light travelling through it should be able to change the matrix shape.*

However, the effect is miniscule and is extremely difficult to measure since photons have very little energy and momentum. Nevertheless, it could be possible that high intensity light should be able to deform it. Recently some theoretical studies have shown the effect of lasers on space-time matrix deformation [114].

Extrapolating on this idea one can conjecture that laser-like *deep thought soliton may deform the space-time matrix just like a mass would do and produce mechanical effects.* This could be the basis of mind-matter interaction [115]. However, the mechanical effect may be very feeble to observe.

The Science of resonance may be able to explain how these effects can be amplified [116]. Also, this interaction of intense thought hologram with space-time matrix may also help in memory formation in knowledge space (KS) .

Resonance Magnification

All systems in the Universe possess natural frequencies and when these frequencies are matched by those of the system creating disturbance, large scale mechanical effects are observed. A classic example is the child on a swing. A slight push (disturbance) to the swing at the right time can make it go higher and higher.

Similarly, certain notes played on musical instruments can shatter wine glasses [117]. In the same manner some of the modern bridges were destroyed when the marching steps of the soldiers on the bridge matched the natural frequency of the bridge.

All these effects show that an exceedingly small force can create large mechanical changes when the natural frequencies of the system are reinforced by a small mechanical force. This is the genesis of Butterfly effect generally described in chaos theory and is an outcome of non-linear dynamics of the system [118].

Thus, we can conjecture that a deep thought-hologram soliton may somehow interact with the space-time matrix in a non-linear way to effect large-scale mechanical changes. We still do not know how this might take place since the natural frequency of space-time matrix is still a mystery [119].

One can speculate that this process may be able to explain the movement of physical objects by thought (psychokinesis) [120] and poltergeist phenomenon [121] where the presence of a troubled person brings in abrupt movements of the physical objects like stones, furniture, etc. Generally, the troubled person is capable of very strong emotional thoughts.

Mahasamadhi or the Final Exit

It may be tempting to speculate whether deep thought soliton may help a person to leave his body by will. Normally death happens by old age, disease or accident [122]. In these cases, the person has no control over the time of exit or how the death will take place. However there have been instances like that of Swami Vivekananda who left his body by will [123].

Sometimes it seems that the physical structure of brain and the body is required to reach the stage of highly non-linear thought and once the soliton is achieved the body's function is over and the liberation of a being from the cycle of birth and death results. Sage Patanjali says that this stage could be achieved by *Dharmamegha Samadhi* (Section IV.29) [124].

I therefore feel that soliton thought wave may be responsible for *Mahasamadhi* of great rishis and enlightened souls which enabled them to leave the body at will guided by the gravity of celestial bodies like sun and stars [125]. This is probably the most economical way energy-wise to leave the gravity of earth.

It is also very tempting to speculate that production of soliton thought artificially and its interaction with space-time matrix may provide a possible mechanism for teleportation and propulsion for overcoming gravity and help in intergalactic space travel!

What is Death and Can We Reduce its Fear?

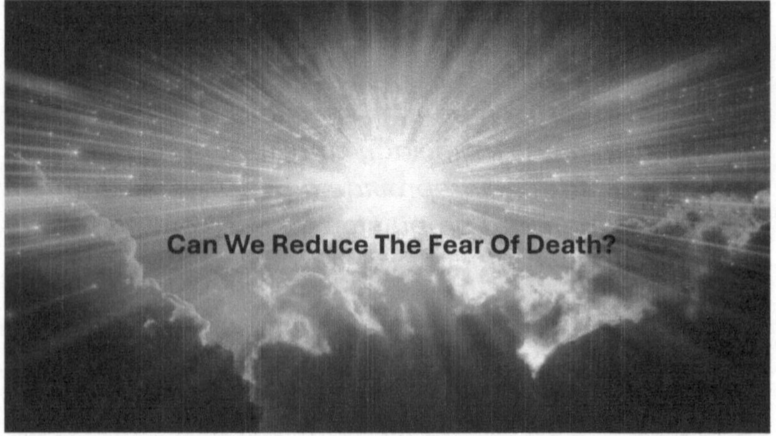

The whole basis of all religions and spiritual teachings is for humans to achieve liberation, moksha, heaven, etc. and get away from the cycle of birth and death on this planet earth.

Death is a very physical process and is the end of the physical existence. Besides it is mostly accompanied by fear and pain. This section analyses the physical nature of this process with emphasis on the emotional and cellular memory removal from the body at the time of death and what can be done to reduce the fear.

At appropriate places the description of death in scriptures is explained in the light of modern science and its principles.

Introduction

Death is the most certain thing for any living entity and yet we know so little about it. It may come earlier or later in life but the inevitable always happens. Yet we carry out our actions and behave as if we are immortal and death does not enter our scheme of things.

In a way that maybe a good thing because the fear of death may not allow us to be bold enough to do lots of things in life. Nevertheless, if we understand the nature of death then we will really understand life, and this will help us to live it fruitfully and happily and not be afraid when the end comes. Reducing the fear of death is the best way to live a happy life.

Through time immemorial in all civilizations, tomes have been written on death. Almost in every society the spiritual writings are about the art of living which prepare human beings for death. *Also, by putting the fear of death in the human beings quite a number of religions and their leaders have exercised control over them by promising better after-life.*

As we grow older death does appear more often in our vision field since this is a part of cycle closure and evolutionary process. Hence a curiosity arose about what is the nature of death; why we fear it and can we reduce this fear.

I wrote my first book "Nature of Human Thought" [1] in 2004 and one of the main chapters in it was on death [2]. It was based on the basic tenet of Indian philosophy and how it pertains to death. Most of the material was therefore heuristic in nature and death was explained in general philosophical terms.

Death is a very physical process and is the final shutdown of the life process leading to the exit of the "self" or memory from the body. Hence, I felt that it should be governed by physical, physiological and neurobiological laws. If we understand these laws, then I feel the fear and pain of death could be reduced. This curiosity and thinking have led to this essay.

Fear of Death

All living entities from the smallest to the largest fear death. *In fact, fear defines an entity as living.* This fear differentiates us from *non-living entities like AI powered beings.* Fear is ingrained in the DNA of all living entities from time immemorial and is a part of the evolutionary process [3]. If there is no fear, there will be no life. *Fear is the engine for the desire to live.* And death completes the evolutionary cycle and is necessary for the evolution and rejuvenation of genetic material. *Thus, fear and death are related and are the basis of life.*

The fear of death comes mainly from three sources: the fear of losing our form [4]; fear of unknown; and physical and emotional pain accompanying it. Loss of form means losing the body and lifetime memories attached to it and this probably produces both emotional and physical pain.

Our memories define us and are the only meaningful possessions we have. Losing them completely at the time of death produces fear. We know deep down that the combination of our present form and with it its unique memories cannot be replicated in any reincarnation and that is why we fear losing it.

In future if by chance, we develop technologies which will keep our memories intact in any reincarnations then the fear of death may be reduced drastically.

The fear of unknown comes because we cannot predict what will happen in future. What will happen to our possessions and to our family is a great cause of concern because we are attached to them and do not want to lose them. With death, all the memories attached to them will be lost and this produces fear of unknown.

The fear of unknown therefore is of present life. We are afraid because we can think about the unfulfilled future possibilities or unknown. Our insecurities give us this fear of the unknown since we can think about them but cannot do very much about them. Nevertheless, once we are gone there is no uncertainty. Hence one of the ways to remove this fear is not to think about death and what will happen to all our memories after we are gone. That could have been the basis of detachment preached in our ancient scriptures.

Fear of unknown also comes from rebirth. Some people say that there is reincarnation and based upon our karma we may be born in different and sometimes unfortunate situations (poor home, in other life forms, etc., etc.) [5]. This uncertainty and unknown future sometimes cause fear.

However, very few people or life forms remember their past birth. Data from various sources of reincarnation study show that the very few who do remember their past births mostly forget about it by the age of 5-6 years [6]. One possibility could be that as the new self or ego starts taking shape (mostly formed at this age) the old memories are forgotten.

Reports also suggest that for those few who remember their past births there is no mention of pain which they experienced either during their early life or during the death [7]. So, all the memories of pain, etc. of past birth are attached to that form and the body. Once the body is gone the pain also goes away and is never carried over to the new body.

Similarly for people who have experienced out of body experience (OBE) or near- death experience (NDE) there is no sensation of pain since it is connected with the physical body and its memories [8]. *Thus, pain and fear of death is a part of the present body, brain and memories.* As long as we have a body there will be a fear of death, triggered by the pain sensation.

Pain

Why is there pain in all living beings? [9]. Pain is a sensation which allows us to take corrective measure for the body repair. Without pain we will not be able to do so. As long as a body and form exist there will be pain. All life forms experience pain: some express it while others suffer in silence.

Bodies of living beings are a marvelous piece of engineering with a self-healing capability. Left to themselves most bodies repair themselves. In most animals when pain comes, they simply try to shut off all activities so that the body auto- repairs it. Modern humans are fast-paced and active, and we want the body to be performing its function without rest; so, we take medicines and other corrective actions like surgery etc. to get it repaired.

The reaction by cells to danger and threat sometimes results in producing inflammation and pain [10]. Inflammation helps in the healing process but sometimes it goes out of hand (nobody knows why), and this leads to runaway events like cancer and tumor formation and other situations where cell production gets out of control. Thus, the pain in the body is an outcome of the inflammation caused by cell death and hence we are programmed to think that death is accompanied by pain. All life wants to avoid pain, and this creates fear. This is also a part of fear of death.

If we can make death painless then most of the fear of death will go away. Modern medicines sometimes help in reducing pain. However, death by sudden mishap like heart attack, accidents, or in sleep etc. is painless.

Emotional pain is an outcome of fear and attachment – losing a loved one, losing a job, breakup, etc. etc. During death emotional pain comes from losing our form and memories to which we are attached while physical pain comes from the inflammation in the body. Interestingly both pains excite the same centers in the brain [11].

It can be conjectured that *during normal death (due to old age, disease, etc.) there is a frantic conversation between brain and body memories since both have to be shed but ultimately the brain decides when to end the existence and that results in brain death.*

However, when the death is sudden and painless for e.g. during sleep, due to accident, by heart failure, etc., etc. it is possible that the body memory does not have the time to interact with the brain which then becomes the overriding entity to decide about the exit. This is very evident in the case of suicides. The body may be healthy, but the brain is distraught and in tremendous emotional pain; and decides to take the drastic action [12]. There are speculations that this may result in ghost formation [13].

Pain Reduction

Most of the pain signals from the body reach the brain through the spinal cord [14]. Ancient Yogis somehow knew how to stop these signals reaching the brain by the practice of *Kundalini Yoga* [15]. This helped in reducing the pain of death. *Kundalini Yoga* is a very difficult procedure to master but the possibility exists [16]. Pain reducing agents or opioids in modern medicines do the same thing much more easily. However, continuous use of opioids leads to addiction and have serious side effects. Data suggests large number of deaths occur because of their overdosage [17].

The greatest effort of mankind should therefore be directed towards developing pain-reduction technologies and systems which are easy on the body and with very few side effects [18]. *If it can be done, then it will be one of the greatest inventions of the world and will have a far-reaching effect on the physical and mental well-being of mankind.* It may well provide the elixir of life [19]. Unfortunately because of greed, big pharma companies all over the world are not putting enough resources into this area [20].

Tomes have been written in philosophical and spiritual literature all over the world and in different civilizations on how to reduce emotional and physical pain. In fact, Sidhartha became Gautam Buddha when he saw an old man suffering and dying and resolved to discover the process by which this pain could be reduced or removed [21]. This is how he discovered Buddhism or the Middle Path.

Since the fear of death is very closely related to the memory of pain, it is instructive to look at the centers of these memories in the body.

Memories of Body and Mind

There are two types of memories in human beings. One is the brain memory which is the sum and substance of all our living experiences and is stored in neural pathways [22]. The other is the memory of form or the body memory which probably resides in cells all over our body and stores life-long experiences of the forces acting on our body [23]. This memory of form is also mapped in the brain. During death both these memories are shed. It is possible that the shedding of brain memory produces emotional pain whereas shedding of body memory produces physical pain [24].

Brain memories are fairly well understood [25]. However, understanding of cellular or body memories is a recent phenomenon and not a fully developed field. I feel cellular memory may play a major role in the fear and pain of death.

Cellular Memory

We exist because of cells. Cells are the basic building blocks of all living things and every part of the body contains cells [26]. There are about 40 trillion cells in human body (including those in the gut bacteria) though the exact number is not known [27]. In comparison the number of neurons in the brain are around 86 billion [28]. *Thus, the cell numbers outnumber neurons by more than 450 times.*

The cells vary in size depending on their function but have an average size of 20-30 micrometers (microns). By comparison human hair is about 20-200 microns thick.

Cells are basically mini factories [29]. They take material from the surroundings and convert it into energy; create new materials (genetic information); create structures like bones and muscles; and replicate themselves. *Thus, they take part in managing every aspect of the body function.*

Cells also have memory [30] which they acquire through the system of epigenome [31], and it can be conjectured that the *combined memories of all cells form the body memory.* Some of the cells also have long term memory [32]. There have been many instances where organ transplantation has resulted in a change of behavior in the organ receiver [33]. Scientists speculate that this could only happen due to body or cellular memory embedded in the organ. We still do not know how the cell memories are formed. They could be a product of rudimentary *"cell neural pathways"*.

Zombie Genes

Then there are Zombie genes in the body [34]. They multiply after the death of the organism, and nobody knows why this happens. It seems the body memory fights death as dictated by brain. We can speculate that this conflict might happen because of lack of equilibrium between what the brain orders and the body's response. Thus, body cells fight death which leads to inflammation and is the cause of pain.

Since cells memories are many times more than the brain memories one can speculate that they might want to have a say at the time of death! Such a thing is probably true because zombie genes do not want to die and in fact help cells to fight death [35].

Brain cells dictate the shutting down of heart and lungs, but body cells resist this shutting down. It is possible that the body cells which give rise to the form of an organism resist the dissolution of form. Why this happens is still a mystery. The form map exists in the brain, but it cannot simply erase it during death. That signal has to come from the cellular memory. *It is the removal of cellular memory which might give rise to physical pain.*

Less than a decade ago researchers debunked the long-held belief that gene expression, which is the hallmark of life, ceases at the time of death. After death zombie genes also activate other genes involved in inflammation, immunity and cancer [36]. So, when organism dies cells rage against the process. Cells don't want to die. *Increase in cancer gene expression in a dead organism infects the organs immediately and could be detrimental to the process of organ donation and transplantation* [37].

Cell Communication

For smooth running of the body, cells communicate with each other to help in growth, development, differentiation, etc. and also to transmit danger signals (for example during cell death) [38]. Besides they also communicate to activate the immune defense system when injury or infection takes place. At the time of death this communication with the brain becomes of paramount importance for shedding and release of memories from the body.

Communication among them takes place mostly by chemical means (by the exchange of molecules through the blood flow). The blood flow is slow, and sometimes the cells need to communicate rapidly for example during death or perception of danger to the body. A possible fast communication channel could be through photonic means.

The exchange of molecules anywhere in the biological system produces bio-photons [39] as a byproduct of chemical reaction and could help the cells to communicate photonically [40]. It is the fastest way for cells to communicate with each other and with other parts of the body.

Memory Transfer After Death

Throughout the history of mankind almost all civilizations have believed in afterlife and reincarnation. Thus, the rituals of burying the dead and mummification were part of this belief [41]. Even in the Hindu religion where the dead body is burnt there is a very strong belief in reincarnation.

We can conjecture that what passes from one body to another is memory [42]. We are not sure what this memory is but could be a basic unit of information. And the transfer could be possible via the process of soliton [43]. Thus, the intense brain activity just at the time of death may allow these holographic memories to be converted into soliton and transferred.

Data from the dying brain shows a heightened activity in the gamma wave region [44]. Interestingly gamma waves (~ 30-100 Hz) [45] are also produced in the brain under very intense brain activity like deep meditation [46]. It is quite possible that this intense brain activity, which is like a *Sanyam* [47], may produce a thought soliton [48]. This could be the mechanism by which memory could be transferred at the time of death and remains stable for some time till rebirth takes place.

Thus, for Yogis, deep thinkers or highly experienced meditation experts who are adept at producing gamma waves the transition during death could be very easy. *It is also interesting to note that gamma waves emission during death has also been seen in rats, and may exist in all life forms [49].*

Reincarnation

There are people who do not believe in life after death or reincarnation and think that after death everything finishes with the body. However, there is strong proof from a large number of cases where there has been a total recall of past lives and events by individuals (especially children) and these cases have been reported in all societies and in almost all religions [50]. Hence, we will take the data of these cases as experiential fact and assume that there are strong possibilities of reincarnation and life after death.

How and where the rebirth takes place is not known and could be purely by chance. Even Patanjali has spoken about it in his yoga sutras [51]. However, for advanced yogis who have mastered the art of intense meditation it is possible that they may be able to decide where they will be born [52].

Interestingly for children who have reported their past births there was no mention of pain or fear of death and in any case those memories are lost by the age of 5-6 years.

Similarly, the fear of death has also been reduced in people who have experienced near death experience (NDE) [53]. NDE seems to happen when a person is declared clinically dead but after some time returns to life. Quite a number of people during NDE episode have reported that their whole life flashed by and almost all their past actions became visible. In majority of the cases after an NDE episode tremendous positive change in attitude towards life and death took place. They were not afraid of death anymore.

Thus, if we think of death and our memories as a part of continuum (as evidenced from NDE and reincarnation episodes) where part of our memories might reincarnate then we may be less afraid of death [54]. However, reincarnation is by chance as Sage Patanjali has stated and could be in any form [55]. When that happens, our memory processing and evolution (depending upon which form we are reincarnated into) may be disrupted. That could also be the cause of fear of the unknown after death.

It is a sobering thought to ponder that nobody really knows what happens to our memories after death. Mostly there are speculations. At best we can conjecture that a basic unit of our present memory passes during rebirth [56]. Therefore many deep discussions in Indian philosophical texts like Mahabharat [57], Upanishads [58], Brahma Sutras [59], etc. have skirted this issue by instructing people to live a good life instead.

Leading a Good Life and Desire to Live

So how does one lead his/her life so that it is happy, and death is painless and is welcomed more like a friend when it comes? Tomes have been written on this subject and the great masters of this world like Christ, Buddha, Patanjali and others have spoken about it from their direct experiences. It will be therefore arrogant on my part to say anything more than what they have already said.

From the present knowledge we can conjecture that to have a good life we must reduce the physical pain by developing wholesome pain management system which provides good health and happiness. Emotional pain can be reduced by living in harmony with nature and all the surrounding forces and practicing spirituality. Spirituality gives us wisdom to curb our greed and use the resources of earth efficiently [60]. Reduction of greed is the best way to create sustainability and happiness.

Most of the times death takes place because of either old age or by accident. In Patanjali Yoga it is written that Yogi who does *Sanyam* on his/her actions and their fructification can predict the time of their death. (Sutra III.23)

I feel that each one of us is born on this planet earth to gain experience. Our collective experiences through different incarnations probably decides the time of death in each lifetime since it is connected to gaining experience. This follows our theory of space closure when experiences of living forms help in closing the cycle of time [61].

A recent interesting study has shown that brain size and longevity are related. Researchers have shown that bigger the brain is longer the life span of that species. It could probably be based on the ability of species with bigger brain size to influence the environment favorably for longer life [62].

I feel it is also related to our desire for experience. When we lose the desire to live (or gain new experience) death takes place. The bigger brain allows us this luxury to decide when we get bored with life. Yet as modern medicines improve and life becomes less painful, we want to increase our experience and live longer. Probably then Patanjali's Sutra III.23 may become useful in predicting the time of final exit.

One of the strongest forces surrounding us is gravity and earth's EM fields. Our body and mind can interact with earth's magnetic and gravity fields [63]. If right from childhood, we are taught meditation and *Sanyam* [64] then it can help us in tuning our bodies to these fields and create calmness and happiness in us so that the brain and body memories are always in harmony and death may not be fearful and painful. This process will also make us live sustainably in this world. We could then rightly be called *Earth People*. Our happy memories which will remain attached to the gravity field of earth after death may then guide us to a brighter future [65].

Since time immemorial mankind has always dreamt of getting out of earth's gravity field and reaching the stars [66]. In all cultures, gods have been depicted as shining beings descending from heaven in flying chariots and blazing machines. One of the reasons could be the desire to get away from the pains and miseries of this planet earth and go to other habitable planets which may provide a better place to live. This could be the basis of concept of heaven preached in almost all religions and could be deeply ingrained in our brains.

We do not yet possess the technology for intergalactic space travel but there are possibilities that we may be able to do so via the soul route and some people believe that reincarnation in other worlds is possible [67].

Nevertheless, a better solution is to make this world of ours a very hospitable place, so it becomes the heaven that our ancient scriptures talked about. Then we may not have to spend time and energy to leave the gravity field of this earth. *Our technological progress should therefore be aimed towards this noble goal.*

How Technology Guided by Spirituality Can Lead to Sustainability and Happiness — A New Paradigm of Development

Introduction

All civilizations throughout the history of mankind have taught the principles of how to live a good and decent life so that the death is as painless as possible. In fact, all religions talk about their method as the best way to reach salvation and in fact all isms (whether religious or political) of the world talk about their path as the best path for leading a fruitful and good life.

In this article I present a new paradigm of development which is based on the combination of spirituality and technology. *This is not another ism* but a combination of existing principles with emphasis on reduction of greed. Once greed for resources is reduced and sublimated for higher thought and greater good, the world can become sustainable, and we can all lead an emotionally satisfying life.

The world is going through tremendous crisis. This includes large scale conflicts and wars and threat of bigger conflict has never been greater that in 1945 (may even lead to World War III) [1]; the shortage of food and malnutrition in large number of countries [2]; unsustainable development leading to worsening environment [3]; economic meltdown in many countries leading to unemployment and widespread discontent among youth [4]; and substantial increase of corruption worldwide [5].

The present state of chaos in the world is a result of excessive greed among the political and economic leaders who want to control the resources and the narrative. If we can temper our greed impulse the world can become a better place to live.

Recently there are world leaders who have taken unilateral decisions without any provocations and without following the due process of law. This may lead to jungle raj and create greater world conflict. Thus, it is necessary to focus on a new paradigm of development which focuses on the moral character of a person, helps in reducing greed and stresses on the universal spiritual values.

This article shows how greed can be tempered and reduced by spirituality which can eventually lead to sustainable development and overall happiness.

Throughout the history of mankind, India has periodically given a new thought to the world. Whether it is Yoga [6], Buddhism, Jainism, Sikhism, Bhakti Yoga or the Non-violence method of Mahatma Gandhi [7]; all have come from India. The world is richer because these lofty ideas and ideals have helped mankind.

I feel another idea can be added to this list. *Technology guided by spirituality can lead to sustainability and happiness.* Basically, *spirituality gives us the wisdom to temper our greed for resources and materials and together with the use of high technology can help us lead a sustainable and happy life.* This essay will detail the thesis behind this idea.

I wrote my first article on this subject 24 years ago [8] and since then have written extensively on it [9] and feel this idea could be a new paradigm of development not only for India but for the world.

What is spirituality?

Spirituality is concerned with matters of spirit. When we think deeply and for a long time about anything whether it is an idea or an object then the brain has a tendency of focusing on it like a laser and in that process the object vanishes from the vision field and only its germ or spirit remains. Then complete knowledge of that idea or object results and is called *Sanyam* by *Patanjali* [10].

This is also the mechanism by which all great discoveries are made [11].

It is this deep thinking on anything which helps us evaluate and resolve the issues and hence removes the clutter from the brain [12]. This makes us spiritual and gives us a sense of peace and happiness [13].

Deep thinking and concentration requires a powerful brain which can be cultivated by continuous and sustained practice [14]. It is preferable that this is learned in childhood since the brain is pliable at that age and has not been cluttered by memory knots. Nevertheless, this practice can be cultivated at any age.

Spirituality is different from religion. Religion is about control. Religious leaders have used it throughout the history of mankind for their own greed – either for power, wealth or fame. It is my belief that all great thought leaders of the world were spiritual – it was their later disciples who converted their thoughts into religion to control and create havoc in the world. Thus some of the largest killings in the history of mankind have been because of religious strife [15].

Spirituality is non-violent and is not concerned about control of anybody but is the search for truth. It is the state of mind that makes it understand that the truth is beyond the barriers of worldliness, religion, rituals, caste, creed, race or geographical boundaries. It makes us look deeper into ourselves and helps us connect to the marvels of nature in a deep way and subsequently to Universal Consciousness.

Spirituality also helps us become fearless since deep thinking helps to resolve the issues which are the cause of anxiety [16]. Fearlessness allows us to chart new paths and helps us become creative and innovative. This also helps us to become contented and reduces show-off impulse and *is the genesis of wisdom.*

Similarly, spirituality also helps us to have a compassionate view of nature and as we evolve spiritually, we become more tuned to it which helps us in preserving it. Besides it helps us to live in harmony with each other and enables everybody to work together for the common good. *This is the genesis of non-violence.* In all religions the respect for nature is preached and the maxim of simple living and high thinking is ingrained in their teachings.

Finally, spirituality also helps us to reduce greed impulse and is the first step towards sustainability and happiness.

Reduction of Greed

The basis of greed is desire. Desire manifests itself in different forms like lust, aim, ambition, control, goal, etc. However, the driving force is the same – power, fame and money and I think it ultimately boils down to control and hence power.

As our brains develop right from our birth, the fast-expanding neuron numbers must form memory pathways [17]. This process is facilitated by sensory perception where the inputs from the senses help us to form the memory. We are therefore hardwired to increase our experience and memories, and this is the basis of desire.

One of the outcomes of desire is possession. We feel a need to possess whatever we desire whether it is a person, object or even an idea. Possession helps us in maximizing experience and gives us a sense of security. As we absorb "experience" through our senses, the brain processes this information. It is during this process that we "decide" whether our desires are fulfilled or not.

Fulfillment of desires through the process of deep thinking and wisdom, therefore helps us in resolving the memories and releasing the "possessions". This results in the feeling of detachment [18] and hence happiness as taught in Gita and Patanjali Yoga Sutras [19].

Unfulfilled desires lead to frustration and increased possessiveness. This leads eventually to more control and greed, which is the major cause of misery and corruption in the world [20].

Rich and powerful are increasing their wealth and power and this is increasing the chasm between rich and poor. With power and through corrupt practices, rich people help create unreasonable laws, which further increases their wealth and their unsustainable lifestyle [21]. Thus, ill-gotten wealth accumulated by corruption is the reason of present strife in the world.

Desire is a useful and necessary emotion. It allows us to achieve something and be active. Without desire we will be lifeless, dead or like stones. Desire and fear are primeval emotions and have helped life to survive by garnering resources and protecting itself from predators. However, what we need to do is to satisfy or channel our desires so that they get fulfilled without too much taxing of resources, materials and energy of this earth.

A powerful processor or the mind can get its desires fulfilled quite easily without physically possessing the objects of desire since it can effectively evaluate all choices and resolve issues regarding consumptive lifestyle. *That is spirituality and it helps us to reduce our greed.*

For example, we can wear only one shirt and one pair of pants at a time, so what is the need to have 100 shirts and pants? Similarly, we can live in one house or drive one car at a time. So, what is the need to have many houses and a dozen cars?

A powerful mind can resolve these issues, reduce the show-off impulse and help us lead a sustainable lifestyle. While on the other hand a weaker brain needs to possess a lot more things for fulfillment of desires, and this leads to greed. *Excessive greed is also the root cause of evil. The killings and lack of empathy by rulers, that we often see in the world, are because of their excessive greed.*

Technological Progress

One of the outcomes of a big brain is that we can modify our surroundings to make our life comfortable. That is the conquest of nature and hallmark of human evolution. *This is also the genesis of technology. The curiosity of how technology works leads to science.*

The history of mankind therefore is the history of technology. Starting from wheel and fire, humans have developed technology to husband resources, energy and materials and to make their lives better and less stressful.

Technology is a double-edged sword. It helps us to live comfortably but at the same time enables us to develop weapons of mass destruction. Technology can be developed and used in whatever way humans want it, i.e. either to help with mankind's evolution or to destroy it because of our greed. Excessive greed itself is bad; but when fueled by technology it becomes lethal. It often leads to wars, monopolies and dictatorships [22].

Yet I feel that technology and wisdom have often gone hand in hand. Though we have developed weapons of mass destruction, the collective wisdom of mankind has stopped us from annihilating each other. The fact also remains that many more people used to be killed in wars when technology was very rudimentary. In today's war fewer human lives are lost.

Most of the wars are resource related and are driven by greed of politicians and that of corporate-military complex [23]. As we advance spiritually and technologically, we will stop waging wars since wisdom will guide us to use resources available more efficiently to provide creature comforts to all of mankind.

I am sure that as *the level of technological progress increases, we will also use it judiciously to further raise our levels of consciousness and not use it to harm mankind.* The power of technology also teaches and spreads the message of moderation through mass communication.

Technology Helps with Spiritual Growth

Technological progress also unravels a lot of hidden areas of nature and shows us how it performs its miracles. In doing this, technology helps us understand the power and greatness of nature. For example, humans felt that they had invented and developed fiber optics. However, scientists have found that the root systems of plants are excellent optical fibers – something that has existed in nature for millions of years [24]. This knowledge could only come once we had enough technology for creating fiber optics, lasers etc.

Similarly, the science of biomimicry or "copy the nature" [25], is developing where we are finding that nature, which has billions of years of head start, has far better answers than we have in almost every aspect of life. Hence realization has dawned that our technological progress will take a quantum leap by copying nature's designs.

In fact, daily we discover that there is nothing new under the sun and all our inventions have been preceded by nature's designs millions of years ago. For example, our computers and artificial intelligence (AI) are following the working of our brains. As our understanding of the human brain and the nature of human thought increases, AI and computing abilities will increase manifold times. With wisdom and reduction in our greed we can also limit the AI capabilities, so that they do not harm us in the long run [26].

Thus, as we progress in the technological area, we will discover the great laws of nature and ultimately God. *For God is nothing else but this marvelous Universe which follows its own scientific laws.* And science and technology allows us to discover the laws of universe and eventually Universal Consciousness. I also feel that it is the law of evolution that as we become more spiritual, we will also become a technologically advanced civilization [27].

This is because when we apply our sharpened brains to any problem, then solutions result. This is the reason why *Patanjali* put the conquest of physical nature (technology) as the third chapter in his book [28] after a yogi became adept in spirituality and control of mind (chapters 1 and 2). *Therefore, a necessary condition for large-scale technological progress is to have spiritual progress.*

The nature of the brain is such that as we make it powerful it wants to increase its inputs and experiences [29]. This is the mind-expanding process which includes peering deep into space and understanding how the world, cosmos and universe functions. This fuels the desire to explore and travel in space and intergalactically. That can only be achieved by very advanced technological progress and is the *genesis of the conquest of space.*

Technology Evolution

Technological evolution will therefore make mankind a galaxy travelling civilization. In ancient times gods came from heaven. *With evolution of our technology, we will become gods ourselves.*

Our technological and spiritual progress can also be explained by giving the example of the path that particles and molecules take in water heated in a container [30]. Each individual particle or molecule darts randomly in the water container depending upon the heat energy given to it but overall, a stream is formed so that the warm water rises, and the cold water comes down to be heated. These are convection cells commonly seen when water is heated or boiled [31]. Individual particles dart furiously in these streams but are restricted by the convection cell boundaries.

Similarly, as individuals we create technologies for our own selfish needs and depending on our spiritual progress may or may not use them for the betterment of mankind. But collectively spiritual and technological progress follows the natural evolution of humans towards an advanced civilization just like the stream of heated water in a utensil. And all our individual shortcomings are swept away for general good by the *convective stream of evolution.*

This evolution is inevitable unless destroyed either by cosmic catastrophe (like a huge meteor colliding with earth and wiping away the life) or by our unsustainable lifestyle and development which can create a critical mass leading to runaway environmental catastrophe.

We feel and enjoy this world through the sense organs of our bodies. Getting a human body is the most important gift to the soul. Almost all technological interventions are to enhance this sense-world interaction. In coming years technology will provide us with tools to create a much more hospitable planet on which majority of mankind will be able to live comfortably. It will help us repair our bodies and produce designer drugs which will make us live longer with less disease and pain.

In fact, the whole basis of *Yoga* according to *Patanjali* is to make the human body fit for spiritual experience and happiness [32]. Our future medicines will allow us to do this. This increased level of physical comfort will allow us a quantum jump in our quest for spirituality and sustainability.

Sustainable Development

Sustainable development means different things to different people but one of the most accepted definitions is "meeting the needs of the present without compromising the ability of future generations to meet their own needs" [33].

However, an excellent definition is what Mahatma Gandhi gave; *"Use resources and materials according to your needs and not for your greed"*.

He himself epitomized simple living and high thinking. All evolved and spiritual people live a simple and sustainable life. *That is their most distinguishing feature.* Sustainability results when we curb our greed and is an outcome of spirituality. Modern examples of evolved humans have been Gandhi [34], Einstein [35], among others who lived very simply and yet produced a very high quality of thought since they were very secure human beings.

The insecurity of humans comes when they cannot resolve issues and think deeply. Thus, activities such as hoarding of wealth, material goods, binge shopping, etc. are the result of a shallow mind and are driven by fear complex of losing out or not having enough. A mind which is very powerful can resolve issues, remove anxiety and find enjoyment within itself to make a person self-contented and happy.

It is a sad situation that the super-rich live a very unsustainable lifestyle. They live in huge mansions, consume enormous amount of energy , resources and materials in a very inefficient manner and fly in their private jets at the drop of the hat [36]. Unfortunately, their unsustainable lifestyle becomes a role model to the general public since these people also own communication networks and mass media and publicize their obscene behavior [37]. Till these people curb their greed their unsustainable lifestyle will continue. They need to imbibe spirituality more than anybody else.

Nevertheless, one can live an emotionally satisfying life with few resources [38]. I have shown this by living in rural India for more than 40 years. In this small experiment I have been influenced by Mahatma Gandhi's definition of sustainability. Thus, by consuming one fourth to one fifth the energy of an average American, I live an emotionally happy and fulfilling life [39]. This example has shown that high thinking and simple living is possible and is necessary for creating a sustainable and just world.

Sustainable living does not mean that you produce everything yourself. But it means that all of us living sustainably can utilize the resources of earth in an efficient manner for a better world. For example, if every person on earth consumes the energy of an average American citizen, then we will need 4 earths to sustain us [40]. This is totally unsustainable.

A simple example of sustainable living is when we live off the interest of fixed deposit in the bank. But when we start using the deposit itself then it leads to unsustainability.

For example, almost all the energy that we humans consume comes from the sun. Even fossil fuels are solar energy stored deep in the earth long ago. Earth's surface receives from the sun about 10,000 times more energy than the whole world consumes [41]. Using it for all our needs will lead to sustainable development. But when we start using fossil fuels, we dip into the fixed deposit leading to unsustainable development.

In the Pursuit of Happiness

All of us aspire to have a good life and happiness. There are as many definitions of happiness as there are people. But generally, people want a decent place to live, mobility, good education for their children, clean environment, a challenging workplace, good and wholesome entertainment and enough money to meet their usual daily requirements. These are the issues around which modern industrial societies have evolved and yet they have created the biggest problem of totally unsustainable lifestyles fueled by greed.

Happiness is a state of mind [42]. We feel happy and enjoy life through our senses and mind. The brain processes the information from the senses, and our level of happiness is dictated by its processing power. A powerful processor can therefore extract more information from sensory signals and hence resolve conflicts in mind. This results in happiness since the mind gets satisfied easily and allows us to be at peace with ourselves [43]. A powerful processor also shifts the priorities in life. Thus, the focus is more on getting mental peace and less on material needs.

A smaller processor obviously needs many more inputs to reach the same enjoyment or satisfaction level. Thus, weaker brains need more resources to occupy them, and this leads to unsustainable lifestyle and unhappiness.

Way forward

How do we create conditions by which this paradigm of development can be propagated?

The most important component in this strategy is to develop a powerful brain. Such a brain allows us to think deeply about everything, and this leads to spirituality and search for truth. A powerful brain also helps in technological development.

Development of powerful brain should start from childhood. Thus, it is very important that we teach our children to focus and inculcate in them the habit of remaining focused on any issue [44]. This will help them get away from Attention Deficit Syndrome (ADS) which afflicts most of the youngsters [45]. Creating such focused youth is an investment in the future of the world.

Naturally this will require very dedicated teachers and school system which will encourage students to think deeply about any issue and be ethical [46]. It is not an easy task but with dedication and effort on our part it is a doable goal. I therefore feel each one of us should become teachers and spreaders of this idea [47]. Slowly and surely, we can inspire the youngsters.

In conclusion the building blocks of this thesis and the new paradigm of development can happen in the following way:

1. By becoming spiritual we can reduce our greed for resources and materials.

2. Spirituality also helps us to be at peace with ourselves and sharpens our brain. Besides, it gives us wisdom and perspective in life.

3. With a powerful brain and heightened consciousness, we can make rapid technological progress.

4. Technology not only helps us to have a comfortable life but allows us to admire the wonders of nature and the Universe and helps with the expansion of our horizon. This is the genesis of space travel and our becoming a galactic travelling civilization.

5. With the wisdom gained through spirituality we will use technology judiciously to use nature's resources wisely and live sustainably.

6. Living sustainably and in tune with nature will give us peace and happiness.

This essay is based on my book "Exploring the Mind of God — How Technology Guided by Spirituality can Lead to Happiness". [27]

The theme of this essay was discussed recently in my talk at Asia's biggest HR conference in Delhi. July 2025 [48].

General Section

Ancient Indian Philosophers Understood Time Just Like Modern Physicists Do

Recently a novel theory in Physics as enunciated by Gunther Kletetschka [1] tries to unite quantum physics and gravity and has been creating waves in the scientific world. If proved correct by scientific community after undergoing rigorous scrutiny, it will change the world as we understand it. In fact, this may be the elusive theory of everything [2] which hopes to capture the workings of the entire universe in a single equation. This was the dream of Albert Einstein and Stephen Hawking.

The major thesis of this theory is that time is three dimensional [3] and is the basis of matter and energy creation. The curvature of time according to this theory produces space, matter and energy. This is very different from Einstein's theory which states that time is a stand-alone entity and interacts with space to form space-time matrix which gets curved by heavy mass [4]. This is the reason why light bends near the huge celestial bodies.

The new theory shows the primacy of time and shows how the birth of the universe took place with the interplay of three dimensions of time. According to this theory the fabric of universe is made of three-dimensional time, and the space is like a paint on this fabric.

This concept tallies very nicely with the ancient Indian philosophical thought where the primacy of time is vividly enumerated.

For example, in Atharva Veda [5] it is clearly mentioned that the world came into existence because of time. "Time is placed in a full pot (Cosmos). Viewing it from various perspectives it has produced all these different worlds". This description of time in Atharva Veda is very similar to what the modern new theory states.

The description of universe formation according to Sankhya Philosophy [6] follows similar lines and states that in the beginning there was nothing and the interplay of Prakriti and Purusha produced the world. Prakriti, according to some Sankhya philosophers, denotes time [7]. And Purusha is Universal Consciousness.

Furthermore, this philosophy states that Prakriti consists of Sattvic, Rajas and Tamas forces which were in equilibrium before the birth of universe and when this equilibrium was disturbed the world came into existence. It can be conjectured that these three forces could be the three dimensions of time according to the modern physics theory and tallies nicely with the Sankhya philosophy.

In Gita also the primacy of time is shown when Lord Kishna shows Arjun his Virat form and utters the famous words "I have become the mighty time - the creator and destroyer of the worlds". Interestingly, this shloka was misinterpreted by Robert Oppenheimer [8] after the atomic bomb blast in 1945 when he quoted Gita stating "I have become Death" instead of I have become the Mighty time.

Similarly, in Patanjali Yoga Sutras [9] Ishwara the supreme being or ultimate reality is defined as an entity which is unconditioned by time. From it originated the world, space and beings.

Some very interesting Sutras in Patanjali Yoga concern space and time [10]. For example, they state that doing Sanyam on moments and sequence of moments a Yogi gets universal knowledge instantaneously and unrestrained by space and time. This matches closely with Einstein's gravitational theory which states "events and interval between events builds space-time". The geometric nature of space-time gives rise to gravity and is the basis of universe and movement of heavenly bodies.

Finally, the primacy of time is also implicit in the last sutra of Patanjali Yoga when it states that ultimate kaivalya or liberation is achieved when mutations of gunas come to their end, resulting in time – the uninterrupted movement of moments to stop.

The comparison of our ancient knowledge with modern science is neither to belittle the latter nor to glorify our ancient tradition – both are important in their own way - but to show that all great knowledge originates from the same knowledge space [11] irrespective of the person and the time of its discovery.

I have always been intrigued by the interaction of gravity with human thought [12] and hence was attracted to this new theory and its implications. November 2025.

How All Great Discoveries are Spiritual in Nature

One of the great Indian mathematicians of last century was Ramanujan. He was a spiritual human being and always said that all his equations and mathematical insights express the thought of God and considered them as a gift from Goddess Namagiri.[1] Hardcore mathematicians scoffed at his metaphysical pronouncements and yet he pioneered number theory and laid its foundation through his theorems which are still being proved and deciphered after 100 years by some of the top mathematicians of the world.

Similarly, the great discoveries of Newton, Einstein, Tesla (the giants of humanity) have all bordered on the metaphysical. Half of Newton's life was devoted to understanding the scientific principles behind God and he devoted a substantial part of his life in writing about them. Einstein also wrote songs about God, which he used to sing to himself.[2] Besides, he was a strong believer in the relationship between science and spirituality. He wrote, "I maintain that the cosmic religious feeling is the strongest and noblest motive for scientific research".[3]

Tesla - one of the greatest inventors of last century - seemed to periodically pluck his inventions from thin air. He always said that most of his ideas came in a flash and the whole machines and their detailed working were "shown" to him.[4]

Similar was the case of Barbara McClintock who had a metaphysical experience and "saw" the phenomenon of jumping genes which later on won her the Nobel Prize in Medicine in 1983.[5] However she was ridiculed for almost 20 years because such metaphysical insights are not considered a part of mainstream science.

It seems that all the great discoveries, inventions and creative outputs like composition of classical music by Bach, Beethoven etc. have been the result of mystical experience. Though most people consider this as a product of a prepared mind, the ideas which are revolutionary and change the course of mankind's history or bring in quantum jump in our understanding, are a product of a nimble brain which somehow plucks the knowledge like magic from knowledge space, especially when no physical proof exists. Sometimes it appears that Gods smile on a chosen few who are blessed with a great idea whether in the realm of philosophy, science, mathematics or music. An element of spiritual connection seems to exist when a great thought or discovery takes place.

Patanjali [1] the great Indian sage has spoken about this connection when he says that any knowledge of the Universe can be obtained by *Sanyam* on it.[6]

Sanyam is a combination of concentration, contemplation and samadhi on any idea. All great discoverers like Einstein, Newton, Tesla, Darwin etc. were endowed with tremendous power of concentration. This together with prepared mind helped them in the discoveries.

The practice of *Sanyam* also points to the fact that those not blessed with nimble brain can produce a powerful prepared mind by sheer hard work.

An interesting facet of discovery process is that most of these great discoverers were self-taught. Their genius flowered at an early age by a single event either by being exposed to a book (in the case of Ramanujan or Enrico Fermi[8]) or to a compass (in the case of Einstein). Such innocuous events triggered in their minds, as if by magic, a tremendous hunger for knowledge.

Also, all these great thinkers talked about oneness of everything. Half of his life Einstein struggled to develop a theory of everything in which he wanted to connect every aspect of universe. Similarly, Ramanujan, Tesla, McClintock etc. all talked about oneness of life, and they all wanted to see the interconnections in everything surrounding us.

With deep thought or *Sanyam* on a particular thing for a long time the brain can become very sensitive and a powerful receiver of knowledge. Such a sensitive brain can identify itself with any idea or object in the world and gets a feeling of oneness of the Universe. Once Shri Ramakrishna, while in a heightened state of awareness, saw a person walking on the grass and felt as if that person was walking on his chest! He had identified himself with the grass as if it was an extension of him. Similar experiences have been given by people who have taken LSD or other hallucinogenic drugs.

Nevertheless, it is the human mind which is the receiver of the idea or knowledge, and there is a curiosity to know what is the mechanism by which it happens.

Knowledge is of two types — internal and external. The internal knowledge is the outcome of memory and information stored in the brain and its churning and processing by *Sanyam*. External knowledge is gained when deep thought interacts with the object of perception. This interaction takes place when the prepared mind produces a thought whose template starts actively matching with the object of perception and with *Sanyam* on it the thought template eventually matches the object in a lock and key type interaction leading to its complete knowledge.

The knowledge about the Universal Consciousness or God or what is the structure of Universe already exists in knowledge space (KS)[7] and is accessed whenever the earth passes through this space in its long journey around the Milky Way. Hence it is time-dependent and not person-dependent. Even if there was somebody else other than Newton or Einstein, they would have received the knowledge provided they had a prepared mind.

It is also the reason why quite a number of people with prepared mind get similar ideas simultaneously and independently. The renaissance period in Europe and spiritual awakening in India in the late 1800s are some of the examples when a large number of enlightened souls pushed the frontiers of knowledge.

As the earth passes through the KS it somehow attracts great thought which comes in human form! This may be the easiest and energywise most efficient way for knowledge seeding of earth.

Thus Christ, Buddha, Ramakrishna, Einstein, Newton, Ramanujan and many more like them were all great spiritual beings who came on this planet earth to increase the knowledge of mankind.

References

1. Robert Kanigel; The man who knew infinity – the life of Genius Ramanujan; Rupa & Co. Calcutta (1992); pg 67.

2. Abraham Pais; Subtle is the lord – The Science and life of Albert Einstein; Oxford Univ. Press, N.Y. (1982); pg 38.

3. Albert Einstein; Ideas and opinions; Rupa & Co, Calcutta (1979), pg 39.

4. Anil K. Rajvanshi, "Nikola Tesla – The creator of the Electric Age". *Resonance*, Vol. 12, No. 3, March 2007 (pg 04-12).

5. Evelyn Fox Keller; A Feeling for the Organism: The Life and Work of Barbara McClintock; W. H. Freeman (1983) http://friends-of-wisdom.com/readings/Keller.pdf

6. B. K. S. Iyenger; Light on Yoga Sutras of Patanjali; Harper Collins Publishers (India) (1993).

7. Anil K. Rajvanshi; Nature of Human Thought (Second Edition); NARI, India (2010); pg 29.

8. Emilo Segre; Enrico Fermi – Physicist; The University of Chicago Press, Chicago (1970); pg 1.

Published in Speaking Tree February 3, 2013.

What is Consciousness?

Since time immemorial mankind has always wondered what consciousness is and where it is located in the brain. Some recent scientific discoveries may provide a possible answer.

There are various definitions of consciousness but the most accepted definition is "awareness" [1]. When a being becomes aware of itself and its surroundings then it is a sign of consciousness.

Awareness is an outcome of thought. It is the thinking brain that makes us aware of our existence and externalities. If we can understand what is thought and where it "resides" in the brain, then we may shed some light on the mystery of consciousness.

It is an accepted fact that thought is produced when brain neurons fire [2]. There are close to 100 billion neurons in the brain (the exact figure is not known). For simple thought like what is the colour of flower, open the door etc. small portions of neurons fire but in deep *Samadhi* which produces *Sanyam* [3] (combination of concentration and contemplation on a single subject or object) almost all the neurons fire to produce a deep thought.

Activation of neural pathways trigger firing of neurons. This activation is caused either by signals from sense organs or stimulation of certain memory space in the brain. Neural pathways help neurons to communicate with each other. During this communication electrical signal from a neuron is converted into chemicals (neurotransmitters) and transmitted across the synaptic cleft (a very small space between neurons ~ 20 nanometers) to another neuron where it is again converted to electrical signal for onward journey.

Scientists have shown that the conversion of electrical signal to chemicals and then again to electrical signal produces weak photons – possibly in synaptic cleft [4]. *I conjecture that these photons from large number of neural pathways synchronize to form a three-dimensional hologram which we can call a thought.* In nature a similar thing takes place when fireflies synchronize their glowing spontaneously to create a signal pattern.

These signals (firing of neurons or fireflies glowing) synchronize spontaneously since they are influenced by each other via a positive feedback-type mechanism. For example in case of fireflies this feedback is through their light signals where they adjust their phases so that they synchronize [5]. In a similar way it is possible that the weak photons produced during firing of neurons synchronize and form a thought-hologram. *This is the genesis of consciousness and internal awareness.*

The synchronization of weak photons is guided by an entity called 'I' (ego, will, etc.) which acts like a symphony director [6] and helps provide the necessary energy and focus to maintain a given thought for a longer time. Ego "I" also compares this thought constantly with signals from outside to provide us a sense of reality. *This is the genesis of surrounding awareness.*

We still do not understand completely how "I" can influence this process, but just like the music conductor who determines which part of the orchestra plays for how long, 'I' decides how long a particular thought will remain in the "vision" field. This process is called concentration and seems to also exist in animals.

Very intense concentration results in deep thought and *Samadhi* [7]. This is a mechanism by which the personal consciousness becomes a part of Universal Consciousness [8].

The production of weak photons for thought formation could also be the reason why many Yogis have experienced seeing white light during intense meditation [9]. Similarly, the observation of white light by persons during near death experience (NDE) could be an outcome of nearly all the brain neurons firing during the final exit.

Since the firing of neurons for a single thought is from different parts of brain there is no single place where we can say the thought originates. *Thus, consciousness exists but one is not sure where in brain it is.* This is just like music which one can never say where it is but when played by musicians exists!

October 2020

This article is an outcome of NATURE discussion on this subject.

Genesis of Fear and How to Reduce It

Fear is the most primordial emotion. Life and fear are interrelated. If there is life it will be afraid because the survival of a living being is very much controlled by fear. It allows the life form to devise strategies and take all the necessary steps to survive and thrive. Thus, fear is inbuilt in us.

Why do we want to survive? It is to procreate, keep our forms, and transfer our genes to future generation [1]; all of these are cornerstones of evolution.

Since it is a matter of survival of living form, evolutionary forces made sure that we are hard-wired for fear. This emotion probably is the earliest and the most important one and hence may use every part of the brain when triggered. Pain is part of fear, and it helps trigger the fear emotion [2] and thus both of them occupy the whole brain during the pain episode.

We still do not understand which neural pathways are excited during the fear episode but one can conjecture that almost the whole brain is involved consciously or unconsciously when a being encounters danger [3].

Hair Raising Experience

I had an experience once of this type of fear in U.S.A. which resulted in the involuntary raising of hair on my neck. It was not by choice or thinking but totally reflexive. In 1987, I was walking in a forested area of Northern Minnesota, USA when I passed a house and out of nowhere three ferocious pit bull terriers and one Doberman came barking at me. I froze at the site of those ferocious dogs and for the first time in my life the hair on my neck stood up.

Those dogs jumped at me while barking frantically and for a moment I thought they would tear me up. However, instinctively I stood my ground, put my hands in the pockets of the heavy jerkin that I was wearing and faced them. They kept on barking and jumping at me. Then slowly I turned and started walking. The dogs kept on jumping at me and barking furiously but I just continued walking unhurriedly.

After a few minutes (which seemed like an eternity) two of the dogs stopped jumping at me and went away. One of the two remaining dogs kept on barking at me while the fourth one just followed me. By squarely facing them probably I sent a message or a thought signal of not meaning any harm to them which removed their fears and made them not attack me. If I had run their chasing instincts would have been aroused and that would have resulted in a really dangerous situation.

I have often thought about that hair-raising experience and thus this essay is a small attempt in trying to understand fear.

I feel that hair acts as an antenna [4] to broadcast the fear signal. All life forms puff up when confronted with extreme danger. Sociologists call it "becoming big response" but I feel the raised hair sends the signals to nearby beings about the danger. We still do not understand the exact mechanism.

Body Map

There is a strong possibility that life forms are born with the body maps in their brain [5]. Since survival is the most important thing this map is the first memory and the genesis of fear and psychological knots.

As we age other memories are formed when inputs from the environment are received through the senses. But the primary focus is survival and to keep the form intact. These memories in turn lead to all other emotions like jealousy, greed, hoarding, anger, anxiety, etc. and are parts of the fear complex [6].

For example, we hoard for rainy days; we have greed for resources and other things so that we do not suffer hardship or pain in future and thus these emotions form a part of our survival strategies.

It can also be conjectured that this original memory of form that we have at birth could also have embedded memories from past births and could be the genesis of reincarnation [7]. Patanjali has written that pain of death is eternal, and the living form remembers it and may inherit it in new body form.

Reduction of Fear

If we can reduce fear – we cannot eliminate it as we may end up losing our form and body; then we can do lots of great things. Fear reduction decreases the psychological knots and makes available the released neural pathways for increasing the processing power of the brain.

In fact, the history of the world is the history of fearless and sometimes fool-hardy people. They charted new paths and territories by going ahead without fear. Some failed and perished but those who succeeded created new thoughts, inventions, discoveries and thus helped in mankind's evolution. Thus Buddha, Christ, Newton, Darwin, Einstein, Gandhi, among others were all fearless individuals who discovered the universal truths.

In Patanjali Yoga [8] it is clearly written that once you remove *Sanskars* or memory knots then true liberation takes place. Thus, total removal of fear is liberation.

Removal of *Sanskars* can be done by cultivating an ability to have deep thought [9]. Thinking deeply about anything gives us the ability to analyze and resolve the issues. This is one of the most effective ways to reduce fear and anxiety. But it requires that we are honest with ourselves and are not afraid to look deeply within.

When we do not do deep analysis then decision-making is influenced by our psychological knots and the actions are impulsive and driven by fear. Such actions are irrational and dangerous and if carried out by people in power they can be lethal. History and present scenario are full of such people— Hitler, Stalin, Mao and now Putin, Xi Jinping, North Korea dictator Kim Jong-un, among others are all examples of rulers who are driven by fear and distrust.

Tomes have been written in ancient philosophical books about reduction of pain but fear reduction is missing in them [10]. In Patanjali Yoga he never talks about fear but only about pain. Since pain triggers the fear complex hence it is possible that Patanjali talked about pain only. Probably removal of pain is partial removal of fear since fear of pain is also one part of the fear complex.

October 2022

Nature of Form – Why Life is Attached to It?

We all identify entities with their forms. Either living or non-living entities are all identified by their physical forms. Our own body-form creates a memory map in our brain, and we identify ourselves and others with those memories.

The idea of form has always intrigued me. If a simple physical and thermodynamical analysis is done on a system, then one faces a dilemma about how to put the energy of form in it. For example, when a body (either a living or a non-living one) gets destroyed then its atoms and molecules all get distributed in space since matter cannot be produced or destroyed except in nuclear fission or fusion; or at very high temperatures when it becomes plasma! Similarly, the energy that goes in making its structure converts into heat and is also dissipated in space. But what happens to the energy of form? And also, what happens to its space-time structure that it displaced for some time in that form?

These are some issues which I think are fundamental to species survival and procreation. *I feel that the fear of death is associated with the destruction of form.* Hence all living entities protect their forms and procreate to provide its continuity.

Darwin in his seminal work "On the Origin of Species" [1] always talked about how all species and living organisms reproduce so that the genetic information is passed from one generation to another and survival of the fittest is tied to this concept of propagation of genetic material. But the central question of why any species has this inbuilt mechanism that it wants to propagate the species or basically its form is still not answered.

Similarly *Patanjali* in his Yoga Sutras [2] says that the desire to have life and the fear of death is eternal but is silent on why it is so.

A possible answer to why it is so can be gleaned from the description of origin of Universe in *Sankhya* philosophy [3].

According to this philosophy the interaction of *Purusha* and *Prakriti* produces matter and the worlds. *Purusha* is described as omniscient, omnipresent, and indivisible entity. *Prakriti* (nature), which is always active, interacts with *Purusha* to produce the worlds.

We can think of *Purusha as multidimensional (MD) space* and *Prakriti as time.* When they work together the creation and evolution of universe and the visible world takes place.

This is similar to the conjecture of some of the modern scientists about the birth of universe. They say that in the beginning, time and multidimensional (MD) space were in equilibrium. The Universe came into being when that equilibrium was disturbed. Why that equilibrium was disturbed we do not know. Various theories abound like big bang, multiverse, brane world etc. but why the big bang [4] took place nobody is sure.

I would like to conjecture on a possible scenario; after the space-time equilibrium was disturbed, time came out and the MD space started "flowing". This flow of space possibly produced gravity and eddies which are the cause of visible matter and galaxies. Eddies are small whirlpools which are formed when anything flows turbulently [5]. These are clearly seen in the flow of water in rivers and canals. In air they produce drag on airplanes which sometimes causes bumpy rides.

Formation of eddies is like a new structure being formed from the chaotic (turbulently) flowing material. According to chaos theory [6] order and form suddenly materialize out of chaos. These structures in chaos theory are called "attractors" and probably gave rise to the matter and form of the visible world. This is what scientists call as production of matter from vacuum [7]. Thus, the visible world seems like a crystallization of higher dimensional space and is the basis of all forms.

Eddy formation is a continuous process, and it is possible that with time more and more space is used up for these structures to form the visible world. The rest of the space remains invisible and could be the basis of dark matter and dark energy [8] that the physicists and astrophysics talk about.

Thus it is possible that the production of eddies and hence galaxies and visible worlds will keep on happening till all the dark space is used up and then the reverse cycle of converting visible world to invisible MD space will commence [9]. This will finally lead to time and space coming back in equilibrium. This is the eternal *Brahmakala* cycle [10]; at the end of which all the life in the Universe is supposed to be destroyed.

According to *Sankhya* this "exhaustion" of space takes place since *Purusha* has "experienced" and has become satisfied though one is not sure what *Sankhya* means by experienced. Same thing is said by *Patanjali* in his *Yoga Sutras*.

Why does the MD space go through the journey starting with inanimate celestial bodies, then to the humblest of living systems and proceeds to evolve into a highly thinking human brain and even beyond? *It is because movement and "becoming" is the only way in which consciousness can exist.*

A system in which nothing is happening is a dead system. The MD space can only "feel" and "enjoy" itself through living systems and thus wants to maximize the number of living bodies. Also a big and powerful brain has the capability of producing mind-matter interaction [11] which can change and manipulate the space-time continuum.

Just like the rainwater starts its journey with many small tributaries and goes through rivers and ultimately to an ocean, the MD space may go through innumerable life forms and may evolve through humans and other more evolved beings.

This follows the laws of thermodynamics in which the system tries to maximize the flow of energy and materials through it with minimum of resistance. The MD space minimizes this resistance by going through billions of life forms. These *life forms fill up the MD space* and evolve till they obtain the power to change space-time fabric so that the closure of space takes place and the cycle continues.

This force to fill up the MD space rapidly is possibly the reason why the living beings want to continuously replicate their forms and fear of death is losing that form.

November 2020

Published in Thrive Global. November 2020.

Why Life? – And its Purpose

Introduction

Charles Darwin [1] in 1860 discovered the theory of evolution and changed the direction of thinking of all scientists. This theory had a profound impact on almost all branches of science since the foundation of how things evolve based upon the forces acting on them was shown for the first time. No wonder Darwin has been described as one of the most influential figures in human history and shares the honors with great scientists like Einstein, Newton, Freud, Kepler, etc.

Since then, millions of books, articles, etc. have been written about how life evolved and the theory of evolution is now an accepted fact. There is also a major program of NASA looking for life in other parts of Universe [2].

But the basic question of why life evolved in the first place has somehow remained unanswered. Was it an inevitable consequence of the forces that existed in the Universe just after big bang phenomenon [3] or was there something else which made life possible?

This essay is an attempt to speculate on these questions and possibilities. There are no definitive answers to this riddle, and our attempt is another speculation.

Why are We Interested in this Question?

Before we speculate on why life, we should ask why we are interested at all in knowing about this process. Humans by nature are curious. Our brains are wired for maximizing the inputs to it and this gives rise to curiosity. Curiosity in turn helps our brains to expand and gives us happiness. The inherent nature of the brain is such that when it works at full capacity it gives us a high and great joy [4]. That is a possible reason why meditation is relaxing and gives happiness. Similarly, a deep inquiry regarding our origins is also worthwhile and enjoyable.

Life Production

Two pathways are possible for how life came about.

a) The first relates to the accepted theory of origin of the Universe which started with the Big Bang.

   After big bang space-time came out and hence gravity (gravity is curvature of space-time). Nobody knows how and why. It seems that the equilibrium of space-time was disturbed which resulted in separation of space and time. Later, when things "cooled" off these two again joined to form space-time continuum [5] that exists today. Scientists speculate that this process started ~ 13-15 billion years ago.

At that time elementary particles and quarks [6] were formed and gravity helped them coalesce to form atoms and ultimately molecules. The probable time of such formation was ~ 11-12 billion years ago.

We can speculate that life probably evolved when molecules of certain critical size resonated with the existing gravity field. We are not sure what the resonance frequency of gravity field was at that time or the critical size of the molecules. This was probably the moment when time also got embedded in those molecules since *sensing of time is the basis of the first principle of life.* The arrow of time moves only in one direction, and it is still an enigma. Even the high priest of time – Albert Einstein did not fully explain [7] it but made the space-time continuum as the central theme of his theory of gravitation.

Our ancients also understood the primacy of time. In chapter 11 when Krishna shows Arjun his *"Virat Swaroop"* and shows the form which is brighter than 1000 suns, he tells Arjun that he has become the Almighty Time – the destroyer of the worlds [8].

So, forming of life was inevitable since it was an outcome of the self- organizing complexity process. This process exists in every complex system where suddenly out of chaos "forms" result. This is also the basis of Prigogine's theory of dissipative structures [9]. It seems that the "form" templates help in crystallization of the material to produce life of different shapes. This process of materialization may have instilled the fear of death in all living beings which helped in their perpetuation.

b) Another pathway could be that life has always existed! It forms (the shape and form) and dissolves just like bubbles in ocean. So, space-time is the universal ocean which gives rise to particles, galaxies and life and they eventually dissolve back into space-time. This is a continuous process. This process is very close to the remarkable vision [10] that the Indian mystic saint Shri Ramakrishna [11] had in late 1800s about the formation of universe. There are speculations that this process may be happening only in our galaxy. Maybe the laws of Physics are different in other galaxies [12].

Force for Life Perpetuation

Once life was formed and different forms came into existence what was the motive or the force to perpetuate life. Some speculate that fear of death helped in perpetuating the form and life. And in this process the genetic material (information) is transferred. *Or in other words information transfer is the most important outcome of evolution.*

But why is there a fear of death or why is there a desire to perpetuate the life form. I think the driving force maybe happiness [13] and not fear!

Happiness results when a being experiences different things and places. This is an outcome of a curious mind. As long as curiosity remains, we learn, and it increases our happiness. Once we have exhausted experiences from our planet, we will travel galactically to increase them. We continue this process until we have gained all the knowledge of the Universe. Then the basis of existence comes to an end and a new cycle begins.

This may explain getting happiness for higher forms of life like humans or in future superhumans with even bigger brains. But how do we explain the evolutionary forces for the lowest forms of life with rudimentary brains.

The interplay of time and space gives rise to the visible world which occupies a certain section of space. This is a continuous process and with time more and more space is used up by these visible world structures. The rest of the space still remains invisible and could be the basis of dark matter [14] and dark energy [15] that the physicists and astrophysics talk about.

This production of matter, life forms and galaxies will keep on happening till the space is "exhausted" or "used up" (though we do not know how much percentage of original space that will be) and then the cycle reverses which will finally lead to time and space coming in equilibrium. This is the eternal Brahmakala cycle where all life is destroyed at its end.

This is also the mechanism by which the information obtained through experiences gets transmitted. In the lower forms of life, it is only through genetic transfer but in the higher forms it is also by other modes like written, spoken, and digital forms.

Just like rainwater, which starts its journey with drops converting to many small tributaries and going through rivers and ultimately to an ocean; similarly, space may go through innumerable life forms of varying complexity including humans and other more evolved beings.

This follows the laws of thermodynamics in which the system tries to maximize the flow of energy and materials through it with minimum of resistance. Space minimizes this resistance by going through billions of life forms. These *life forms fill up the space* and evolve till they obtain the power to change space-time fabric [16] so that the closure of space takes place and the cycle continues.

This exhaustion of space takes place since all life forms have experienced, have become satisfied, and achieved maximum happiness. Similarly, Patanjali in his Yoga Sutras [17] says that the cause of visible world is to satisfy the Universal consciousness!

April 2024

Published in South Asia Monitor, 12 April 2024.

Science of Pranayama

Pranayama [1] means regulation and control of prana or breath. It is one of the major tenets of Indian Yogic System. The first definition of *Pranayama* was given by Sage Patanjali in his Yoga Sutras (sutras II:49-53) [2]. He also identified prana as breath and nothing else. Nevertheless, lots of commentators and practitioners later on defined it as a vital force, cosmic energy, etc.

I feel prana is the air we breathe which consists of particles, molecules, microbes, viruses, or any other material in the air surrounding us. And its physiological interaction with our mind and body is the real meaning of prana.

A minute portion of the air we breathe goes to the brain directly via the olfactory bulb [3] – a section above the nose which gives us the sense of smell. This input to the brain tells us immediately about the nature of the environment. Depending upon this input, brain then sends appropriate signals to the various parts of body to take necessary action. If brain senses danger, then auto-immune system is activated and if not then the system does not do anything, and the body is relaxed and helps sometimes in producing serotonin [4] (the happiness molecule) giving us a sense of well-being.

Nanoparticles Reaching Brain Directly

Medical researchers discovered for the first time in 1941 that small amounts of fine particles that were inhaled through nose could be lodged in the brain by breaching blood brain barrier (BBB) [5]. This barrier isolates the brain from getting outside infections [6]. However, this field of research remained dormant till 1990s when scientists, alarmed by rising environmental pollution, visited the early research and started discovering the harmful effects of toxin invasion of brain through breathing.

Recently researchers have also shown that nanoparticles (particle size of 10-30 nanometers which are almost 10-20 times smaller than those emitted in cigarette smoke), can directly reach the brain after breaching the BBB [7].

The majority of air that we breathe however goes to our lungs and helps in producing energy by interacting with the molecules of the food we eat. The waste product of this interaction is the carbon dioxide which has to be expelled. Both these functions; inhaling oxygen and exhaling carbon dioxide are done by the lungs.

This is similar to internal combustion (IC) engine which takes in oxygen to combust the fuel and throws out carbon dioxide as flue gas. Through this process IC engine produces power. Similarly, the gas exchange in our lungs also produce energy [8] which is the source of power through our muscles. Probably this could be the basis of prana as life force.

When we inhale pure air then the conversion efficiency in our lungs is high. It reduces when we inhale polluted air [9]. Thus, inhaling air from good and happy surroundings gives us a sense of well-being. We get this feeling when the environment is pristine and without any pollutants and also when we smell very pleasant and fresh air. Thus, the air we breathe changes our mood and subsequently our body and this probably gave rise to the meaning of prana or life force!

All life forms have evolved so that the signals from surroundings are first sensed by the brain either by olfactory lobe or by specialized receptors like forked tongues in reptiles [10]. After their receipt the brain then sends appropriate messages to different parts of the body.

This is possibly the reason why nose and mouth are on the face and near the brain. Otherwise, a simple engineering design of the body, purely from the utility point of view, would have put the nose next to the lungs and mouth near the stomach!

The superior natural design which took millions of years to evolve made all the external inputs (from ears, nose, mouth, eyes) first go to the brain which assesses the situation so that appropriate signals by it could be sent to the rest of the body for necessary action.

Beneficial Effects of Pranayama

One of the Pranayama techniques is breathing in from one nostril and breathing out from other – also called *Anulom Vilom* [11]. Scientists have found out that breathing through one nostril affects the part of the brain on that side [12], and thus the practice of inhaling through one nostril during *Pranayam* is to stimulate that side of the brain and not for cleaning the nostril as explained by experts in *Pranayam.* Similarly, deep slow breathing allows enough time for the nanoparticles or *Pran* to pass through the BBB and into the brain.

Often the practioners of Pranayama claim that it helps them calm their nerves and gives them a sense of well-being. The reason is that the act of pranayama allows us to easily focus on breathing and this focus on anything for considerable time is meditation. Patanjali also states that Pranayama helps in concentration. Besides different Pranayama exercises also help the lungs, nasal cavities and general well-being.

Many studies all over the world have shown the beneficial effects of pranayama and meditation [13]. Even when it is done in polluted environment [14] it helps though the benefits are reduced. Therefore, when it is practised in a pristine environment the feeling of well-being increases manifold times.

So how does breathing affect our mind and body? A minute quantity of what we breathe in goes directly to the brain via the olfactory lobe. These particles, microbes, viruses, etc. somehow change the communication among the neurons which allows the brain to send appropriate signals via the vagus nerve alerting the rest of the body. The exact mechanism of how this happens is not known.

Such signals in the long run therefore condition the body. Thus, people who live in a pristine environment and breathe fresh air have healthy mental and body make up. People who live in polluted environments and breathe unhealthy air have more problems with their mind and body. This was probably the reason why yogis in ancient times preferred pristine atmosphere of Himalayas.

Nevertheless, if *Pranayam* is practiced in clean and open-air environment daily then it can negate the problems of modern life. A possible mechanism is explained below.

Purifying Air through Solar Energy

It has also been known for quite some time now that

antibiotics-resistant bacteria gets neutralized with fresh air and plenty of sunlight [15]. Researchers are finding that the enclosed environment of hospitals and offices with air conditioning and artificial air breeds bacteria which create diseases in the people residing in these buildings.

Exposing them to plenty of sunlight and fresh air has brought down the incidence of disease drastically. A possible mechanism for this is that UV radiation of sunlight interacts with nanoparticles in air and produces antioxidants and when inhaled have tremendous therapeutic value [16].

In the mountains the proportion of UV rays in sunlight is higher than in the plains and with higher altitude and less pollution the creation of free radicals also increases. Thus, mountain sojourn has always been recommended for improving health. Probably that could also be a reason why *Rishis* and *Yogis* went to mountains for meditation and practicing Yoga.

There is therefore a need to create and use indoor air cleaners [17] which can duplicate the mountain air conditions inside rooms in cities so that Pranayama can be done easily.

Recently scientists have also found out that good deep sleep helps in flushing out the toxins from the brain [18]. Since deep sleep is like meditation detoxification through *Pranayam,* good sleep and meditation can be a basis of healthy brain [19].

Fragrant Smells Help *Pranayama*

One of the most important parts of breathing is

smell. It is perhaps our most memory-evocating sense. The smell signals from the nose go directly to the limbic system-the seat of emotions. Thus, smells evoke deep emotional responses and memories.

Studies have also shown that fragrance can change moods and influence judgment [20]. That could possibly be the reason why throughout the ages, humans have always had a love affair with flowers and their fragrance. Beautiful flowers are not only balm to our eyes, but their fragrance is food for our soul. No wonder fragrance and perfume is 30-35 billion dollars industry today [21]. Mood enhancing incense has been used in religious practices in almost all societies through immemorial times.

Thus, the clean crisp mountain air with a whiff of pleasant smell from flowers literally evokes the abode of gods since *Pranayam* in such an environment provides the mechanism for detoxifying and cleaning the brain for better meditation and hence liberation. Even in our daily life, we can do *Pranayam* in open and clean air.

For a healthy planet we need to improve the air quality wherever we live. We can then inhale pristine air or prana and live a healthy and fulfilling life.

How Sinuses May Help in Humming

In 2020 at the height of COVID pandemic, I started doing Neti [1]. It is an old yogic practice of cleaning the nose and the sinuses. One puts lukewarm water in one nostril by the spout of the Neti pot, and it flows out by gravity from the other nostril. This is done a couple of times. It cleans up the nose and keeps the sinuses healthy.

Sinuses are the first defense against airborne diseases and COVID-19 which spreads through air was supposed to be taken care of by Neti [2]. During the pandemic I did not get COVID. Whether it was due to Neti; or living in a clean environment; or strictly following COVID protocols (including vaccination); or good immunity; one cannot tell.

However, one of the unintended benefits I observed, as I progressed in Neti *kriya* (practice), was that I could hum nicely. During my student days in IIT Kanpur [3] in late 1960s I used to practice singing and had attained some proficiency. Later on, I stopped singing but this cleaning of nostrils and sinuses allowed me to start it again.

I therefore felt that probably the basic function of sinuses in human beings is to make the brain resonate when we hum or sing [4]. And the use of sinuses as a first defense against airborne diseases could be an evolutionary progression. Many researchers have speculated on why we have sinuses but it has still remained a mystery [5].

Sinuses or empty spaces in skeletal structure help in reducing the weight of the birds for flying purposes but in humans it does not make sense to have them for this purpose. I therefore conjecture that it might be to vibrate the brain when we sing, hum or chant in a certain way. Doing this is very enjoyable and I am sure singers in different cultures might vouch for that.

Why does such humming produce an enjoyable feeling [6]? I think a probable answer could be that when the vibrations reach the brain it helps in "jiggling" the neurons so as to produce better connectivity for neural pathways. Or in other words these vibrations may help in increasing the firing of neurons similar to that when we take some drugs. Brain plasticity can be increased either by chemical, physical or photonic means [7]. Nature uses all the forces that act on any system for increasing its efficiency and brain is no different.

Ancients understood the power of these vibrations, and it can be conjectured that Sanskrit [8] language may have come out of this understanding since chanting of Sanskrit mantras produce lot of humming vibrations. It is therefore quite possible that humans evolved with singing as primary means of communication; languages evolved later on.

Not only humming may help in improving neural pathways formation, but it might also help in stimulating the vagus nerve. Studies have shown that vagus nerve stimulation affects the voice [9] and so by principle of equivalence singing and humming may stimulate vagus nerve.

Sinuses and thoracic cavity probably form a total resonance system. Both of them have to be clean for resonating at some natural resonance frequency. We are still not sure what this resonance frequency is; but some call it Brahma Naad [10].

The maximum vagus nerve fiber density is in the thoracic region [11] and its vibration by humming or chanting in deep lower notes may help in its stimulation. Stimulation of vagus nerve is very necessary for keeping a healthy body and mind. Many studies of vagus nerve stimulation [12] have shown that it helps in regulating heart rate, keeping the gut healthy and in toning of the nervous system.

In different cultures chanting or singing in deep lower tones has been a part of religious or mindfulness practices and the above scientific principle may help explain the practice. Thus, if we keep our noses clean it will help us to remain healthy and be happy!

Published in South Asia Monitor, 6 January 2023.

Lessons from India's Spiritual Tradition

India has produced some of the greatest spiritual thought of mankind. The ancient spiritual thought was very scientific in nature and based on deep inquiry of truth. The *Upanishads*[1], *Patanjali Yoga Sutras*[2], *Bhagwat Gita*[3], etc., are part of that great tradition.

The ritualistic tradition of Hindu religion came later on when the spirit of inquiry degenerated. This degeneration of thought however provided an impetus for rejuvenation of India by creation of new thinking in the form of Buddhism[4], Jainism[5], Sikhism[6], etc. It was as if the old spiritual thought was washed and made clean by these new developments.

The degeneration of great thought took place when rulers started controlling people. Spiritual thought got converted into religion which allowed the rulers to control people and resources, and the rituals and associated systems of the religion helped to increase this control.

Rituals help to create fear which makes it easy to control a person. For example, the rituals like, you have to pray so many times; have to give so much *prasad* to the temple; wear this ring or the bracelet; give so much material to a pundit are all part of the mechanism to control the person. Fear is put in the minds of people that if you do not perform the rituals then major calamity will fall on you. Fear is a powerful mechanism to control people.

Throughout the history of mankind all "isms" are used to control population, whether it is religions or a system of governance. The authors of new thoughts did not control. It was their followers who used their ideas to create isms for control. They put fear either by physical or mental means. In the present scenario the fear of pandemic also came in very handy to a lot of dictators and rulers to control the population. This fear creation (either real or fake) by rulers throughout history helped them to divide and rule.

By nature, a very powerful brain will always seek the truth. The ultimate truth is beyond caste, creed, color, country, etc. Old *rishis* who developed India's great spiritual thoughts lived in a rich and beautiful country like India and were endowed with very powerful brains. Once their basic needs were satisfied their minds soared to understand the universal truths. Thus *Patanjali*, authors of *Upanishads*, *Gita*, etc. were seekers of truth.

The ancient Indian spiritual thought always encouraged spirit of enquiry [7]. The guru helped the disciple by pointing and guiding him/her to the goal; the disciple then followed it based on his degree of application. There was no control exercised, just the guidance given. It is this spirit of enquiry and seeking truth that is presently missing in our society. Somehow it has to be inculcated in our children and young adults. India has always progressed economically, culturally, and emotionally when it pursued the path of spirituality and search for the truth.

Thus, it can be conjectured that the general prosperity in ancient India followed after a new spiritual thought came. The Mauryan empire, especially Ashoka [8], followed after Buddha; Harshvardhan empire [9] was inspired by Adi Shankaracharya [10]; Chola dynasty [11] and the rise of the great Hindu Kingdoms of Southeast Asia including Angkor Wat[12], came after Sage Ramanuja[13].

This inspiration is visible in the wonderful architecture of the temples. I have always wondered about what forces shaped the lives of the workers who made the temples which took years to make— some even more than hundred years. It was not simply a paid job but a part of great thought and a mission which inspired and guided the workers. This made them proud of their creation and allowed the flow of high quality of craftsmanship.

In the recent past, work of NASA space program [14] followed this process. More than building the rockets it was the desire to win the space race against Russians and a greater desire to conquer space - the next frontier, that drove a lot of people to do wonderful work in NASA.

I also feel that the great thought of Mahatma Gandhi [15] of non-violence and adherence to truth, which had fired the whole of India to win our independence, would have helped produce a great economic activity in the country if we had not followed the socialism route. After all Gandhiji inspired industrialists like Birla, Tata[16], Bajaj[17], etc. to help in Independence movement and nation building and I am sure they and other industrialists would have continued with even greater vigor in this task if they had been allowed freedom to do so.

Similarly, the desire in each Indian to help build the newly independent India was very strong and when that desire did not get a proper outlet in the socialist structure then the enthusiasm slowly faded.

This can have some lessons for the present dispensation. Instead of following the unsustainable growth example of U.S. and China which is based on extreme greed and very materialistic outlook, we should follow our great philosophical and spiritual tradition and give the world a new direction of development based on the mantra of *"high technology guided by spirituality can produce sustainable development and happiness"* [18].

Epilogue

India has produced some of the greatest spiritual thought of mankind. The ancient spiritual thought was very scientific in nature and based on deep inquiry of truth. The *Upanishads, Patanjali Yoga Sutras, Bhagwat Gita.*, etc., are part of that great tradition.

As an engineer I have always looked at the scriptures and ancient Indian philosophical thought from a scientific point of view. The spirit of enquiry and my scientific training have helped me in this pursuit.

As I have read deeply in some of the scriptures (it is not possible to delve in all of them – one lifetime is not enough for such an exercise), I have found some scientific gems in them and those I have highlighted in the book. The starting point has been Patanjali Yoga Sutras (PYS). The science embedded in them is really remarkable and it has been very enjoyable to study and interpret them.

I feel such an exercise might also help us find new scientific laws, inventions and discoveries. That is the reason why we are interested in reading these scriptures and interpreting them in the light of modern science and technology knowledge.

Very often one feels a desire to look at the ancient texts and subjects from the modern perspective. Isaac Newton spent half his life trying to decipher Bible from the perspective of his scientific knowledge at that time.

Similarly, we are fascinated by great works of Panchatantra; those by Chanakya, Kalidas, Shakespeare and try to see how they fit in our present scheme of things. The value of ancient books becomes manifold when they can explain the situation in modern world. This was the motive of writing this book.

Nevertheless, the comparison of information in scriptures with that in modern science is neither to glorify our ancient tradition nor to belittle the latter – both are important in their own way; but to show that all great knowledge originates from the same knowledge space irrespective of the person and the time of its discovery.

All the material presented in the book has also helped me develop a new line of thinking and a mantra: Spirituality + Technology = Sustainability and Happiness. I feel this provides a new paradigm of development not only for India but for the whole world and was mostly inspired by my understanding of science in ancient Indian scriptures. In fact, this is one of the central themes of the book.

One of the greatest traits of ancient Indian philosophical thought was the spirit of inquiry and search for truth. This allowed the ancient gurus to show the way to the disciples and not impose their isms. This is a great lesson from our ancient scriptures and the gems of science in them reflect that noble tradition. Science has no ism. Therefore, if we follow our ancient philosophy true to its spirit rather than the presently followed jingoistic based religion, then we can make India a holistic, sustainable and a nice place to live in.

I hope the readers have enjoyed reading the book. It is also my hope that they may be inspired to undertake their own study of ancient texts in the light of framework outlined in this book.

Acknowledgements

I am deeply indebted to my elder daughter Noorie Rajvanshi and my wife Nandini Nimbkar for discussions, advice and editing. I am extremely grateful to Namita Gokhale and Sunita Bansal for facilitating this book's publication by Motilal Banarsidass International. Thanks, are also due to our intern Ms. Sweta Rani for creating reference database and to Shri S.S. Aherrao for typing the articles.

About the Author

Dr. Anil K. Rajvanshi has more than 42 years of experience in renewable energy R&D and rural development. He did his B. Tech and M.Tech in Mechanical Engineering from Indian Institute of Technology (IIT) Kanpur in 1972 and 1974 respectively. He received his Ph.D. in Mech. Engg. from University of Florida, Gainesville, USA in 1979 under solar energy pioneer Dr. Eric Farber. He was on the faculty of University of Florida (Dept. of Mechanical Engineering) for 2 years before returning to India in 1981 to run his own rural NGO – Nimbkar Agricultural Research Institute (NARI) in Phaltan, Maharashtra.

NARI has done pioneering work in agriculture, renewable energy, and sustainable development, especially those affecting rural population. Dr. Rajvanshi has devoted the last 44 years at NARI to apply sophisticated science and technology to solve the problems faced by the rural people in the areas of energy, water, pollution, and income generation;

broadly based on use of renewable energy in environmentally sound ways.

Dr. Rajvanshi has written extensively on his work on rural self-sufficiency. He has more than 350 publications; eight books and chapters in various books; and 7 patents to his credit. He has been inducted into several prominent committees of the Government of India (GOI) at the national and state level. He is the principal author of the Govt. of India national policy on Energy Self Sufficient Talukas.

For his work, Dr. Rajvanshi has received a number of prestigious national and international awards, such as Jamnalal Bajaj Award; induction to the U.S. based Solar Hall of Fame; Austria based Energy Globe Award; Federation of Indian Chambers of Commerce and Industries (FICCI) Annual Award; Sweden based Globe Award; Distinguished Alumnus Award from University of Florida (he is the first Indian to receive this award); Padma Shri (one of the highest civilian awards from GOI); Distinguished Alumnus Award from IIT Kanpur; Legends of IIT Kanpur; among others.

He has been a featured speaker at many prominent institutes, conferences, and forums, both in India and abroad and lectures regularly on the issues of sustainability and rural development.

Besides his engineering work, he is also involved in studies of human consciousness and the interaction of spirituality and technology. His writings on these issues have appeared regularly in Times of India; Huffington Post; Thrive Global; South Asia Monitor; among others. He has also written three books on these issues.